THAT'S WHAT
THE MAN SAID

THAT'S WHAT THE MAN SAID

The Sayings of Jesus

Maxie Dunnam

UPPER ROOM BOOKS®
NASHVILLE

That's What the Man Said

No part of this book may be reproduced in any manner whatsoever without written permission of the publisher except in the case of brief quotations embodied in critical articles or reviews. For information, write Upper Room Books®, 1908 Grand Avenue, Nashville, Tennessee 37212.

The Upper Room® Web site: http://www.upperroom.org

UPPER ROOM®, UPPER ROOM BOOKS® and design logos are trademarks owned by the Upper Room®, Nashville, Tennessee. All rights reserved.

Scripture quotations not otherwise identified are from the Revised Standard Version of the Bible, copyright 1952 (2nd edition, 1971) by the Division of Christian Education, National Council of the Churches of Christ in the United States of America. Used by permission. All rights reserved.

Scripture quotations designated KJV are from the King James Version of the Bible.

Scripture quotations designated AP are the author's paraphrase.

Excerpts from "Being Children of the Kingdom" by John Killinger, which appeared in the July/August 1983 issue of *Pulpit Digest*. Copyright © 1983 by *Pulpit Digest*. Used by permission of Harper and Row, Publishers, Inc.

Excerpts from "Anyone for Calvary" by Charles R. Woodson, which appeared in the April 1965 issue of *Pulpit Digest*. Copyright © 1965 by *Pulpit Digest*. Used by permission of Harper and Row, Publishers, Inc.

Excerpt from "Savior by Storm Light" by William A. Ritter used by permission of the author.

Excerpt from "The Duty to Be Happy" by Mark Trotter used by permission of the author.

Excerpt from "Nothing Can Hold You Back" by Norman Neaves used by permission of the author.

Excerpt from "God and the Poor" by J. Ellsworth Kalas used by permission of the author.

Excerpt from the following sermons by Donald J. Shelby used by permission of the author: "Making Today Count," "Dateline for Decision," "Incognito," and "Speaking of Hallowed Things."

"Two Friends" Copyright © 1970 by David Ignatow. Reprinted from POEMS 1934–1969 by permission of Wesleyan University Press.

Excerpts from "The Christ of the Resurrection" by Samuel Shoemaker in *20 Centuries of Great Preaching*. Copyright © 1971 by Word Books, Dallas, Texas. Used by permission of the publisher.

Excerpt from *The Communicator's Commentary*. New Testament Series. Volume 4. Copyright © 1983 by Word Books, Dallas, Texas. Used by permission of the publisher.

"Sometimes, We Take the Initiative in Prayer" by Loretta Girzaitis originally appeared in *Alive Now*. Used by permission of the author.

Cover design: Jim Moore
Book design: Harriette Bateman
Cover transparency: C. Aurness / West Light
Ninth printing: 2001

ISBN: 0-8358-0599-9

Printed in the United States of America

Contents

Introduction

Somewhere I read of an art show with a unique introduction. The entry area of the gallery featured what appeared at first to be four paintings. Actually, the paintings were on mirrors. As you looked at them your mirrored image was what became dominant. The arrangement was an imaginative statement about the nature of art; it was an invitation to enter the paintings—not to remain aloof as an indifferent observer, but to identify.

That's my invitation to you as we look at some of the sayings of Jesus. It is the nature of scripture that we are to put ourselves into it. We are to be participants of the drama, not spectators.

Under the rubric *That's What the Man Said*, we are going to look at some of Jesus' sayings. These are

> tough sayings,
> demanding sayings,
> comforting sayings,
> bracing sayings,
> judging sayings.

Perhaps all of the sayings will be familiar to you, but I urge you to read them as though you have never read them before. Look with new eyes and listen with a fresh heart. Do you remember Robert Burns's challenging word?

> Oh wad some power the giftie gie us
> To see oursels as others see us!

Jesus' words help us in that important task of seeing ourselves as we really are. In the fifth book of C.S. Lewis's *Chronicles of Narnia: The Horse and His Boy*, the boy Shasta finally meets the great lion Aslan (a Christ figure) and learns from Aslan the amazing story of Shasta's own young life. Aslan tells the story and his part in Shasta's beginnings and his journeys. He helps Shasta understand what Shasta's story means. Shasta then asks Aslan to explain the meaning of some of the experiences of his traveling companion, Aravis. But Aslan responds, "I am telling you your story, not hers. I tell no-one any story but his own."

So Jesus does. As he speaks and as we listen, we hear our own story. As we respond, we find the direction we need to live as God intends and/or as Christ calls.

There is a sense in which this is a workbook. There will be a running narrative in one column, consisting of reflection and commentary on a particular saying of Jesus. In another column on each page, there will be a lot of blank space for you to write your own questions and record your own thoughts. There will also be guidance for your reflection, questions to ask of the text and to ask yourself, occasionally some additional material for reflection, and space for you to write your responses.

Your writing can become a sort of spiritual journal as you see yourself in the mirror of Jesus' word. The book will be most meaningful as you participate in the reflection/writing process. When you come to this symbol ◇ with an accompanying number, such as *1.* or *2.* in the narrative, then go to the adjoining column and respond to the suggestion there. After doing so, return to the narrative.

Following the last chapter, you will find a guide for group discussion which will be helpful if you choose to use this book with a Sunday school class or for any small group experience.

Quotations from most sources other than scripture are followed by the author's name and page number on which the quote can be found. These citations are keyed to the Notes section at the back of the book where you will find complete bibliographic information.

Welcome now to the gallery of *That's What the Man Said.*

CHAPTER ◇ 1

Violets Cracking the Rocks

Tennessee Williams was one of America's greatest dramatists. In their commentary about his life and work, critics often made the point that he was a lonely and frightened man. His plays presented a world of shattered hopes and failed visions. While he loved his characters, they, like him, struggled against the frightening blindness of their lives.

Later, Williams became less angry and frightened. After his death, Dan Sullivan, writing in the *Los Angeles Times*, noted that Williams's themes had changed; that in his later work, he was writing about "the power of violets cracking the rocks."

That's a powerful image—"the power of violets cracking the rocks." More powerful, but in the same category, is Jesus' image in our text: "Consider the lilies . . . how they grow; they neither toil nor spin; yet I tell you, even Solomon in all his glory was not arrayed like one of these." Jesus closed this section of the Sermon on the Mount, his lesson about God's care for us, with the admonition "Don't be anxious."

That's What the Man Said. If God's lilies of the field, by simply being what God created them to be, don't have to toil or spin in order to grow; if God clothes the grass of the field, which has such a tenuous life—today, it is; and tomorrow it is cast into the oven—if God can put enough power in such a fragile violet that it will break through a stone in order to breathe the air and find life—why are you men and women, whom God has made a little lower than the angels and crowned with glory and honor, so faithless?

Don't be anxious! *That's What the Man Said.*   ◇ 1.

We need to hear this word of Jesus because ours is a fear-ridden day. We would be naive not to register that fact as we seek to listen to Jesus.

Russell Baker of the *New York Times* is one of my favorite writers. He did a tongue-in-cheek piece for *Life* magazine (August 15, 1969) which he titled, "The Good Things That Undone Poor Gum." It read in part: "They buried Gumbacher last week. The death certificate said he died of *coliosorus gravis*, more commonly

◇ 1.

Therefore I tell you, do not be anxious about your life, what you shall eat or what you shall drink, nor about your body, what you shall put on. Is not life more than food, and the body more than clothing? Look at the birds of the air: they neither sow nor reap nor gather into barns, and yet our heavenly Father feeds them. Are you not of more value than they? And which of you by being anxious can add one cubit to his span of life? And why are you anxious about clothing? Consider the lilies of the field, how they grow; they neither toil nor spin; yet I tell you, even Solomon in all his glory was not arrayed like one of these. But if God so clothes the grass of the field which today is alive and tomorrow is thrown into the oven, will he not much more clothe you, O men of little faith? Therefore do not be anxious, saying, 'What shall we eat?' or 'What shall we drink?' or 'What shall we wear?' For the Gentiles seek all these things; and your heavenly Father knows that you need them all. But seek first his kingdom and his righteousness, and all these things shall be yours as well. Therefore do not be anxious about tomorrow, for tomorrow will be anxious for itself. Let the day's own trouble be sufficient for the day.

—Matthew 6:25-34

known as the spreading decline, but his friends know better. Gumbacher was slowly scared to death by the combined efforts of several thousand national campaigns to help him live longer. At the end Gumbacher simply had more terrors weighing upon him than the human body can support . . . Every day science was discovering that something Gumbacher had been exposed to all his life was lethal." Everywhere he turned he was bombarded by dire predictions that he might be coming down with a dozen different fatal conditions. He finally concluded that all he could do was die. When someone mentioned his plight to scientists, they replied, "If more people in this land had the good sense to be afraid of living, they would live longer." We can all identify with Gumbacher; it seems as if everything we pick up carries warnings about the possibility that what we are taking into our bodies might be harmful to us.

◇ **2.**
List here three things that you worry most about.

◇ **2.**

Ours is a jittery age, but the problem is that we are worried about the wrong things. We are terribly worried about success and prestige, but we're not worried half enough about what we're doing to ourselves. We ought to be bothered about ulcers and heart attacks that we bring on ourselves. We ought to be bothered about the fact that our friendships are superficial. We ought to take note of the fact that no amount of money can compensate for the way we rob ourselves and become slaves to ourselves. So one of our problems is that we worry about the wrong things.

We have a right to be anxious. Conflicts and upheavals around the world are moving our nation deeper and deeper into a war mentality. That's reason for concern.

AIDS, which some are describing as a modern Holocaust, is a disease that seems destined to claim millions of lives. In 1987 one out of 61 babies born in New York City tested positive for the AIDS antibodies and the figure is escalating. By the year 2000, it is predicted that many millions of persons will be infected with the AIDS virus worldwide.

That's a part of the big picture, and it is anxiety-producing; but we don't have to think at that level. Our day-to-day living brings enough. Jesus knew that, so he said, "Therefore do not be anxious about tomorrow, for tomorrow will be anxious for itself. Let the day's own trouble be sufficient for the day" (Matt. 6:34).

I was looking through some old journal notes recently and came across a page I had written back in 1975. I wrote it in a hospital room when I was recovering from an automobile accident that had left me with a broken leg, two broken ribs, and a collapsed lung. I was reflecting upon all that had happened in a brief three months. I share it as I wrote it then.

For Everything There Is a Season

How much life can be packed into such a brief space?

August 12—   my forty-first birthday. Over forty now—
                   past that magic center. Few references to
                   "that young preacher."

August 15—   Selected as nominee for editorship of *The Up-
                   per Room*—a pinnacle of professional achieve-
                   ment;
                   a platform for expansive ministry of worldwide
                   dimension.

September 17—   the shocking news—Lloyd's death. My
                   forty-three-year-old brother—
                       died heroically trying to save others,
                       Death had never been so close.
                       I couldn't remember my grandparents'
                   death;
                       I remember my grandmother faintly, but then
                       death hadn't registered on me.
                   But this was my blood brother—two years
                   older;
                   the one who had shared my childhood.
                   We had grown apart—
                       teen years,
                       college . . . military . . . family
                       a continent apart
                   but now we were *near* again;
                       the relationship was growing.
                       He'd been in our home the weekend before.
                   Now—dead.

October 6—   fiftieth anniversary, the golden year for
                   my mom and dad.

November 15—   Crack!
                   Two cars head-on.
                   Here I am in the hospital,
                   Broken leg—broken ribs—collapsed lung.
                   Three months!
                       How much of life in ninety days.
                       Life . . . death . . . success . . . joy . . .
                       anguish . . . celebration
                       Crushed bones.

How we know it! There are enough troubles in each short day, certainly in the short span of our life, to verify the perspective to which Jesus is calling us.

One of the important things Jesus is saying is this: *Don't borrow trouble.* I don't know the history of that phrase, but I know what it means. So do you and so did Jesus. "Therefore do not be anxious about tomorrow, for tomorrow will be anxious for itself. Let the day's own trouble be sufficient for the day."

Let's look at that issue from two perspectives. One will immediately strike a chord in us; the other, we have probably thought little about.

First, *don't borrow trouble by taking on excessive anxiety about things you cannot change.* Excessive anxiety about things we cannot change is one of the biggest issues in our life. Let me share a letter I received after a sermon in which I talked a bit about this sort of thing.

> Dear Maxie:
>
> I couldn't let the week go by without expressing to you how much your sermon meant to me on Sunday. For the past few months, I've really been in a valley. Life has just burdened me down. Business problems which have plagued us for over a year; bills that never seem to get paid; expectations that seem like faraway dreams. I've known how I was supposed to feel, how my faith was supposed to give me strength, but in reality I've been depressed to the point of making myself physically ill. Christmas was an attempt to do the right things, say the right things, and pretend that everything was "great." I had grown weary of pretending.
>
> To add to my depression [my son] decided not to go back to college and moved with no notice to an apartment. It broke my heart. He and I are very close, and the thought of his leaving home was something I was not prepared for. I felt disappointed that he was not in school, not pursuing a career, not the yuppy son of so many of my friends.
>
> Your sermon made me take a good look at myself, and my "feel sorry" attitude. In reality, I cannot be responsible for my son's decision. He is twenty years old—and probably one of the most respectful, loving, caring people I know. God has a plan for his life. Thanks for reminding me to turn him over to God.

That person has come to a good place; she is freeing herself of excessive anxiety about things she cannot change. There are some burdens that we cannot handle for ourselves, and there are some burdens that we were never meant to handle. Those burdens are to be turned over to God. That's the reason I like the Serenity Prayer of Alcoholics Anonymous:

> God grant me the Serenity to accept
>   the things I cannot change,
> Courage to change the things I can;
> And Wisdom to know the difference.

So, Jesus is saying, don't borrow trouble by taking on excessive anxiety about things you cannot change.   ◇ **3.**

Now, a second perspective on hearing Jesus' word: "Don't be anxious." *Don't borrow the trouble of worrying about your ability to live the Christian life.* This is something most of us have thought little or nothing about. Yet, I think it's a big problem in many of our lives. We worry about our ability to live the Christian life.

Recently, I counseled with a psychologist who thirteen months before had been freed by God from a crippling drug addiction. He was thankful for his deliverance, but he was almost paralyzed by fear that God was going to place calls upon his life to which he would not be able to respond.

Worrying about our ability to live the Christian life is a big problem for many of us. That's one way it expresses itself. The other way is anxiety about the fact that we will fall into sin again.

We know that we are weak and that we do give in to temptations. Our problem comes when we adopt a "poor me" attitude that says, "It's always going to be like that. I'm simply not able to live the Christian life."

To be sure, we sin. Hopefully, we feel guilty for our sins. But we must not remain in our guilt. Scripture promises that when we confess our sin, God forgives and "remember[s] our sin no more" (Jer. 31:34).

Here is what we need to remember. *It is adding sin to sin if we choose to remain guilty after confession and repentance.* We can exchange our guilt for praise because "the blood of Jesus his Son cleanses us from all sin" (1 John 1:7).

So we don't borrow the trouble that comes from saying, "I'm sure I'll do it again. How can I ever be delivered from this besetting sin?" As Christians, we are *in Christ*, and we must live believing that *in him* we live one day at a time. We don't dwell on the possibility of succumbing to temptation tomorrow. Jesus has set us free now. Now, not tomorrow! As far as tomorrow is concerned, Christ is our keeper. We are living in him; and as long as we do, he will keep us. So don't borrow trouble by worrying about your ability to live the Christian life.   ◇ **4.**

Jesus' word about not being anxious suggests a third important truth: *The greatest price we pay for worry is the loss of the richness of living today, this very day.*

I like T. S. Eliot's poetry, even though I have to struggle to read and understand it. The truth that he expresses is worth the arduous effort and energy we might invest in reading him. One of his geniuses is his creation of power-packed phrases and images. In his "The Dry Salvages," there is this line: "For most of us, there is only the unattended Moment."

There's the gripping image: "the unattended Moment."

◇ **3.**
Do any of the three things you listed on page 10 as those things you worry most about fall into the category of "taking on excessive anxiety about things you cannot change"? If so, pray now that you will be able to yield those things to God.

◇ **4.**
Check again the list of three things about which you worry most. Is any one of them a fear about living the Christian life or doing what God may call you to do?

Reflect further. Write two or three sentences about your failure to receive Christ's forgiveness and/or your fear that God may call you to something to which you will not be able to respond.

That's what all of life becomes for us when we don't hear what Jesus said: "Don't be anxious about tomorrow."

If fear of tomorrow or the day after tomorrow consumes us, we will miss the possibilities of today. In his sermon "Make Today Count," my friend Donald Shelby tells of one person who, awakening to how dingy his life and world had become because of his worrying, made a worry table. Analyzing how he and other people worried, he concluded that 40 percent of most worries never happen; 30 percent were about past decisions that we cannot alter; 12 percent about criticism (mostly untrue) of us by others, usually arising from envy and misunderstanding; 10 percent were about personal health that only grew worse with worry; and only 8 percent were legitimate concerns that need our attention. All of this, according to Don, means that when we worry we waste a lot of time and energy, and overlook opportunities which may never come again to us, special moments that may occur only once in our lifetime. "Think of the hugs that we have shunned because we were worrying, the spontaneous surprises of children growing up, the wayside miracles in nature, the fun of playing together, the secrets that we could have known, the beauty we could have shared."

The unattended moment is packed with possibilities for richness, meaning, and growth. But we miss it because we are not focusing our eyes on the present and are anxious about tomorrow.

I think one of the most meaningful reflections upon this out of my own life was the result of an experience I had many, many years ago when we lived in Anaheim, California. I shared this experience in my book *Dancing at My Funeral*. When our children were growing up, we did some things with them out of a sense of duty and with great effort, but our trips to Disneyland did not fall into that category. We lived only about ten minutes from Disneyland, and we went at least twice a year. Despite my familiarity, I always entered Disneyland with a keen anticipation, and I never disappointed. On one of our family's visits, I was standing there in the Magic Kingdom, gawking at this monument to human imagination and technological abilities, when two women walked right into me!

"Pardon me," I said. They didn't even see me! I don't think they saw *anything!* They were knitting!

I don't knit, but I appreciate this craft, and I enjoy wearing knitted sweaters. I do confess that I have this "thing" about people who knit when I'm speaking—I have doubts about anyone concentrating on two things at one time. But these women could knit while walking! (Until people like me got in their way.)

While these women impressed me with their knitting ability, I'm afraid that they totally missed the magic of the Magic Kingdom. And while I hope that they finished those sweaters or shawls or whatever, I also hope that someday they'll return to

Disneyland *without their needles and yarn* and permit themselves
to be thrilled by the Magic Kingdom.

I've poked a bit of fun at women knitting, but even in these
days of a renaissance of arts and crafts, nobody is likely to scold
me—*except myself!*

> Lord, I don't know why those ladies
>   were knitting so intently.
> There was so much to be
>   wide-eyed at.
> I wonder if they missed any stitches?
> Knit one, purl two.
> The shawl emerged,
>   but they missed the "Magic Kingdom."
>
> Wow!
> That's what I've done.
> I've missed the Magic Kingdom—
>   *the kingdom of now.*
>
> I missed it by being
>   so preoccupied with the past.
> The "hound of hell"
>   demanded all my attention.
> Why haven't I realized
>   that his bark was worse than his bite?
> The bark was the frightening thing.
>   So I ran
>   I fought
>   I whimpered.
> Then remorse set in—
>   resentment
>   regret
>   bitterness
>   guilt.
> All my energy was required
>   running from
>   or fighting
>   that "hound of hell."
> Knit one, purl two,
>   and I passed through the now;
>   missing the Magic Kingdom.
> The future robbed me, too.
> I closed my ears to the hound's bark
>   and listened to tomorrow's siren song.
> Stars were in my eyes
>   getting out of Richton
>   graduating from college
>   finishing theology school

moving to the next church
earning more money
gaining professional status
publishing that first book.
The sparkling stars of tomorrow
blinded me to
balmy sun
mystic moon
dashing waves
love-lighted eyes
inquisitive frown
knowing smile
awareness.
Knit one, purl two,
and I passed through the now
missing the Magic Kingdom.

Forgive me, Lord,
I heard
but I didn't listen.
I looked
but I didn't see.
"The Kingdom is *at hand*."
"The Kingdom is *within you*."
"*Today* is the day of salvation."
"*Now* is the acceptable time.
NOW . . .
the Magic Kingdom
knit one, purl two?
Forgive me, Lord.

◇ **5.**
You don't have to have a bizarre experience such as being run into by women knitting to remind you of losing the richness of living today.

Write your own confession of failure to live now.

Don't forget it: The greatest price we pay for worry is the loss of the richness of living today ◇ **5.**

Now a final word: *We can trust God for tomorrow, because we can trust God for today.* Hear clearly Jesus' words: "But if God so clothes the grass of the field, which today is alive and tomorrow is thrown into the oven, will he not much more clothe you, O men of little faith?"

A member of our congregation and a dear friend, Roger Watson, knows this truth as well as anyone I know. We can trust God for tomorrow, because we can trust God for today. Roger is an alcoholic, but Easter Week, 1989, he celebrated eleven years of sobriety. He remains sober because of his one-day-at-a-time-trust in the Lord. He wrote a contemporary gospel song which expresses this truth in a memorable way. The title of the song and its message are a simple prayer Roger heard an old man pray: "Lord, we know what you're gonna' do 'cause we see what you've already done."

Go back to my beginning image, violets cracking rocks. It's a powerful picture. A tiny, fragile violet with so much life in its tiny structure, with so much thrust for sunlight and air that it literally cracks the rock and pokes through so that it can peek at the sunlight and finally burst forth in its pristine purple glory. Paul said that nothing in all the world can separate us from the love of God which is in Christ Jesus. You see, we can trust God for tomorrow, because we can trust God for today.

My friend who wrote me the letter from which I quoted earlier, closed by saying, "You were right—this is a new year. I filled up several trash bags since Sunday. As Ralph Waldo Emerson said, 'What lies behind us and before us are small matters compared to what lies within us.' I know that I have the Holy Spirit within me. He will give me the strength to overcome this depression and to trust him this year."

So it is. So it will be! "What lies behind us and before us are small matters compared to what lies within us." We have the power, like the violet, to crack all the rocks of circumstances. So listen to what Jesus said: "Don't be anxious about tomorrow!"   ◇ **6.**

◇ **6.**

In reflecting on this message of Jesus, Harry Emerson Fosdick reminds us that "our lives fall into two parts: first, the things we can get by direct attack—when we want them we pounce upon them as a lion on his prey—but second, the ends which must be gained by indirection. Some things we achieve as we catch a railroad train, by running after them, but some things are not like that—they come of themselves when their conditions are fulfilled."

Go back and read Jesus' word for this chapter (Matt. 6:25-34). Spend time reflecting on these questions. Write notes about your reflections.

1. Is my lifestyle characterized more by attempts to get what I want by "direct attack" or by a willingness to cultivate the soil, plant seed, and *wait for the harvest*?

2. Am I more anxious about "eating and drinking" and "what I wear" than I am about the plight of the homeless in my city? Do I worry about *the wrong things*?

3. What is the one big thing that I cannot change about which I have excessive anxiety?

CHAPTER ◇ 2

Destiny Is a Matter of Choice, Not Chance

◇ **1.**

He went on his way through towns and villages, teaching, and journeying toward Jerusalem. And some one said to him, "Lord, will those who are saved be few?" And he said to them, "Strive to enter by the narrow door; for many, I tell you, will seek to enter and will not be able. When once the householder has risen up and shut the door, you will begin to stand outside and to knock at the door, saying, 'Lord, open to us.' He will answer you, 'I do not know where you come from.'

Then you will begin to say, 'We ate and drank in your presence, and you taught in our streets.' But he will say, 'I tell you, I do not know where you come from; depart from me, all you workers of iniquity!' There you will weep and gnash your teeth, when you see Abraham and Isaac and Jacob and all the prophets in the kingdom of God and you yourselves thrust out. And men will come from east and west, and from north and south, and sit at table in the kingdom of God. And behold, some are last who will be first, and some are first who will be last."

—Luke 13:22-30

◇ **2.**

Locate in your memory an experience in your life when you took the easy rather than the hard way, and it led to disaster. Write enough about that experience to get it clearly in your mind. Use the space at the top of the next page also.

Destiny is a matter of choice, not chance. No one illustrates this better than Jim Abbott. He was born with only one hand and has taught himself to pitch baseball. He has a dexterity that those who watch find remarkable.

Sports Illustrated reported that he "delivers ninety-mile-per-hour fastballs, not to turn doubters into admirers or the curious into the awestruck. His objective is to turn batters into outs."

At the time I read his story, Abbott was a sophomore southpaw at the University of Michigan with a 10–3 pitching record. "He says, no, he's not discomforted; no, he's not courageous." He doesn't even consider himself handicapped. "I'm a pitcher working at it," says the 19-year-old from Flint, Michigan, "and people write me letters calling me an inspiration." Abbott has always counted his good fortune and never dwelled on his misfortune. "I've been blessed with a pretty good left arm and a not-so-great right arm," he says.

Jim Abbott sums up the secret of his life by saying, "I had to learn to do it with one hand, because that's all I had."

Destiny is a matter of choice, not chance. *That's What the Man Said.* Pay attention to him: "Enter by the narrow gate; for the gate is wide and the way is easy, that leads to destruction, and those who enter by it are many. For the gate is narrow and the way is hard, that leads to life, and those who find it are few" (Matt. 7:13-14). ◇ **1.**

"The gate is wide and the way is easy, that leads to destruction." Here is the commonplace suggestion that vice is more attractive than virtue. Is Jesus saying that the line of least resistance is commonly the way of disaster? ◇ **2.**

Jesus is tough in sounding the result of such directionless, undisciplined living. *Destruction* is more than physical death; it is eternal punishment—complete death as opposed to eternal life. T. W. Manson in *The Sayings of Jesus* described it as "death with no hope of life as opposed to life with no fear of death."

Jesus recruited no one by false pretenses. Everyone knew

exactly what they had to reckon with if they were to follow him. We will look at this again, especially in chapter 11. Here Jesus makes it scathingly tough. The narrow way of self-denial and self-sacrifice is not the popular path that most wish to walk. To walk the narrow way demands firm determination and constant effort. Only a few will remain on the way. Those who do, find life—eternal life.

Someone asked the late Sam Ervin before the Watergate hearings if he were ready for such a responsibility, the burden that was placed upon him. He replied, "I've been preparing for this moment all my life." That illustrates the meaning of this theme of Jesus: Destiny is a matter of choice, not chance.

Register, first of all, that *this is a lesson about choosing. Life is life by the choices we make.*   ◇ **3.**

Life is made up of the decisions we make, and our decisions reveal our inner natures.

In an essay on "The Divided Self," William James wrote: "There are persons whose existence is little more than a series of zigzags, as now one tendency and now another get the upper hand. Their spirit wars with their flesh, and wayward impulses interrupt their most deliberate plans."

Isn't that an apt image? The zigzag life. Unfortunately, too many of us live that kind of life—a life that is drawn now this way and that. Contending desires are always warring in our lives; allowing that war to rage dooms us to failure. A person without a purpose is like a ship without a compass or course.

Choosing the narrow gate is the set of the sails of our life. You remember that old poem:

> One ship sails East and another West
> with the self-same winds that blow;
> It's the set of the sails and not the gales
> that determines the way it goes.

If choosing is the set of the sails of our life, *discipline is the wind that moves our boat on its chosen course.*

One achieves the abundant life Jesus offers only by discipline. Bishop Fulton J. Sheen once said, "The difference between a river and a swamp is that the river has borders and the swamp has none." That's a picture of discipline—having borders to our lives.

We all know that there are choices that restrict and diminish life. The Danish philosopher and religious thinker Sören Kierkegaard had a story about a wild duck flying south with other ducks. Below him in a barnyard he noticed some corn the farmer had scattered for his tame ducks. The duck broke formation with his wild friends and joined the tame ducks in the barnyard. He ate the corn, liked it, and decided to stay a few days. The corn was free and life was easy, so he stayed longer. Spring came, and it was time for the wild ducks to fly north. One day, high overhead, the duck heard his wild mates calling as they flew by. Their call reminded him of

◇ **3.**
The choices we make, for the most part, either restrict and diminish life or enhance life and broaden its possibilities. Test this in your own experience.

List here and write a sentence or two about choices that have restricted or diminished your life.

Now, list and write a sentence or two about choices that have enhanced your life and broadened its possibilities.

4.

Harry Emerson Fosdick asked this question: "What are the prerequisites of greatness in any realm?" then answers: All of them in Jesus' sense of the word, are narrow. *Attention* is narrow. When Gladstone was asked the secret of his success he replied in one word, "Concentration." The worthwhile mind can focus, but the inattentive mind sprawls every which way. *Decisiveness* is narrow. We cannot decide vaguely and in general; we must decide in particular. The decisive mind defines, excludes, wills this and not that, but the indecisive mind is a vagabond on a broad road. *Loyalty* is narrow. It binds me to a definite devotion. When I love my friend I am not loosely free; I do not wish to be loosely free; my limitation is my glory; I love my friend. But the unloyal man travels a broad road; he has no attachments; he is devoted to no friend; he is a man without a country—broad is the gate and wide is the way." (Fosdick, *Living Under Tension,* p. 205)

Write a paragraph about attention, decisiveness, or loyalty leading you to freedom.

his true life, but when he tried to join them, he could not fly. No flying and too much corn in the tame barnyard had claimed his strength. He had stayed on the ground too long.

An athlete who does not practice soon loses his ability to perform well in competition. A musician who refuses to rehearse soon has nothing to rehearse for.

To have freedom in doing something, whether in sports or the arts, one must be disciplined. Tenacity and persistence are key factors. Scientist Louis Pasteur said, "Let me tell you the secret that has led to my goal. My strength lies solely in my persistence."

Playwright Noel Coward said, "Thousands of people have talent. I might as well congratulate you for having eyes in your head. The one and only thing that counts is: Do you have staying power?"

So, choosing sets the sails of our life, and discipline is the wind that moves our boat in its chosen course. Bishop Ernest A. Fitzgerald, writing in *Piedmont Airlines,* rightly reminds us that "a business person who is interested only in today's business will not be doing business tomorrow. A person who places no value on integrity and trust will be trusted with less and less. People who use their friends have no friends to use after a while." ◇ **4.**

Register another truth: *Discipline and keeping clear our purpose can clothe even a weak person with power*. John Wesley's motto was "This one thing I do." It was the key to his long life of service. Nothing swerved him from his purpose. He taught the early Methodist preachers the same lesson when he said to them, "You have nothing to do but to save souls."

It was no different with Martin Luther. Discipline and purpose gave him power. "If I had heard that as many devils would set on me in Worms as there are tiles on the roofs, I should none the less have ridden there." No wonder he had the power to say, "Here I stand. I cannot do otherwise."

So when we discipline ourselves and keep clear our purpose, we claim power not available in any other way. Jesus was not suggesting a requirement for us that he had not responded to himself. "My meat," he said, "is to do the will of him that sent me, and to finish his work" (John 4:34, KJV).

When a man wishes to become a member of the Benedictine monastic order, he is accepted on probation. I've been told that during the first year, the street clothes which he wore to the monastery are hung in his cell where he can see them every day. At any time, he can take off his monk's habit, retract his vow, and walk out. Only after a year are his old clothes finally taken away. By then he knows whether his commitment is deep enough, whether his discipline and purpose have given him the power to keep his promise and follow through on his vow.

So, what Jesus said is a lesson about choosing. *Choosing* is the set of the sails of our life, and *discipline* is the wind that moves the boat of our life on its chosen course. It is discipline and purpose that can clothe even a weak person with power.

Let's go back now and pick up on an earlier theme which we mentioned. Choosing the narrow gate is an urgent issue because it determines eternal life or death.

Luke puts this word in a different context than Mark. "Strive to enter by the narrow door; for many, I tell you, will seek to enter and will not be able," Jesus said. Then he uses the metaphor of people knocking on a door, saying, "Lord, open to us." But the Master of the house will say, "I do not know where you come from" (Luke 13:22-30).

All of this came in response to the question "Will those who are saved be few?" The assumption of the questioner was that only Jews would get into the kingdom of God; Gentiles would be shut out. Jesus' answer was shocking. Entry into the kingdom was not automatic; it came to those—*all those*—who diligently struggled to enter.

There will be surprises in the kingdom. The people in Luke's story who knocked and were refused entry said, "Why not? We ate and drank in your presence, and you taught in our streets." Still they were turned away. Being a part of a "Christian nation" is no passport to the kingdom. Being a church member is not a ticket to the kingdom.

Choosing the narrow gate is urgent business. So Kierkegaard reminded a friend: "Do you suppose that life will forever suffer itself to be treated as a joke by you? Do you suppose that, like Cinderella, you can slip out a little before the midnight hour?"

Alexander Maclaren reminds us that Jesus' exhortation to "enter by the narrow gate" is followed by two clauses, each of which begins with *for*. One is a description of the road to be followed and the other of the path to be shunned. In each description there are four contrasted particulars: the gate, narrow or wide; the road, narrow or broad; the travelers, many or few; and the destination, life or destruction.

Then Maclaren makes this significant point:

Now, people generally read these words as if our Lord was saying, "*Though* the one path is narrow and rugged and steep and unfrequented, yet walk on it, because it leads to life; and *though* the other is the opposite of all these things, yet avoid it, because pleasant and popular as it is, its end is destruction." But that is not what He says. All four things are reasons for avoiding the one and following the other; which, being turned into plain English, is just this, that we ought to be Christian people precisely because there are difficulties and pains and sacrifices in being so, which we may ignobly shirk if we like. It is not, *Though* the road be narrow it leads to life, therefore enter it; but *Because* it is narrow, and leads to life, therefore blessed are the feet that are set upon it. (MacLaren, p. 222)

That leads to this final truth: *Destiny is a matter of choice, not chance. That's What the Man Said:* "Enter by the narrow gate," or door. Door? What door? Jesus also said, "I am the Door." Listen to his full word: "I am the door of the sheep. All who came before me are thieves and robbers; but the sheep did not heed them. I am the door; if anyone enters by me, he will be saved and go in and out and find pasture" (John 10:9).

Choice and discipline are not to restrict life but to expand it, to make it abundant. By me, as the Door, Jesus said, "(you) will go in and out and find pasture, and (you) will be saved."

Roger Fredrikson is the pastor of First Baptist Church in Wichita, Kansas, and the author of the volume on John in *The Communicator's Commentary.* In that commentary, he talks about the eight years that he has served in that courageous inner-city congregation, watching with amazement as the Great Shepherd has gathered his flock—"many of them, it would seem, sheep not of this fold, but hearing His voice and coming."

Roger testifies that out of the wounds of a terrible church split more than twenty years ago, the Lord is creating a new people—a strange, wonderful mixture of the curious, the seekers, and the needy, joining with a faithful remnant, to go in and out, finding pasture.

> One of these was Anna—frizzy-haired and anxious, coming forward at the invitation every six or eight weeks in some service of worship to let us know how desperately she wanted to be a part of His flock. Her childhood life had been filled with anger and trouble. Now two of her sons were in the state penitentiary, one for life, and her daughter was in alcoholic treatment. Anna always seemed to call our home during mealtime or late at night, either to vent her hostility, "I'm never coming back to that church again," or to confess her love for all of us, "I don't know what I'd ever do without that church." What joy it was to watch our people, at first cautiously, but then freely, accept her as one of us. Anna has since died, on the operating table, as the surgeon was trying to repair her stomach, badly damaged by a bleeding ulcer. She represents so many needy, dispossessed, neglected people who have come to us in these last years.
>
> When Bob and Pat, who live five miles east of the church, began worshiping with us, I could not resist asking after some weeks, "Why in the world would you attend First Baptist when many of your tennis-playing and social friends belong to a strong, suburban church?" Bob's answer was classic, "We want to be a part of a church that treats Anna the way First Baptist does." And so they joined! As Jesus said, "They will hear My voice; and there will be one flock and one shepherd." (Fredrikson, pp. 183-184)

Jesus is the door. If we enter by the narrow gate—and that door, which is Jesus—if we make that choice and allow the wind of discipline to lead us in the direction of the choice that we have made, then we will go in and out and find pasture. Destiny is a matter of choice, not chance.

Life calls for selectivity. While we are doing one thing, we can't be doing another. When we say *yes* to Christ, we must also say *no* to other things, so we can be true to the biggest *yes* of our life.
◇ **5.**

◇ **5.**
Recall and describe the narrowest gate through which you have had to walk to life.

List the areas of your life, such as use of time or money, sexual gratification, or eating habits, where you are least disciplined.

Write a prayer of commitment, surrendering these concerns to Christ.

CHAPTER ◇ 3

God Has No Grandchildren

◇ 1.

Now there was a man of the Pharisees, named Nicodemus, a ruler of the Jews. This man came to Jesus by night and said to him, "Rabbi, we know that you are a teacher come from God; for no one can do these signs that you do, unless God is with him." Jesus answered him, "Truly, truly, I say to you, unless one is born anew, he cannot see the kingdom of God." Nicodemus said to him, "How can a man be born when he is old? Can he enter a second time into his mother's womb and be born?" Jesus answered, "Truly, truly, I say to you, unless one is born of water and the Spirit, he cannot enter the kingdom of God. That which is born of the flesh is flesh, and that which is born of the Spirit is spirit.

Do not marvel that I said to you, "You must be born anew. The wind blows where it wills, and you hear the sound of it, but you do not know whence it comes or whither it goes; so it is with every one who is born of the Spirit." Nicodemus said to him, "How can this be?" Jesus answered him, "Are you a teacher of Israel, and yet you do not understand this? Truly, truly, I say to you, we speak of what we know, and bear witness to what we have seen; but you do not receive our testimony. If I have told you earthly things and you do not believe, how can you believe if I tell you heavenly things? No one has ascended into heaven but he who descended from heaven, the Son of Man. And as Moses lifted up the serpent in the wilderness, so must the Son of man be lifted up, that whoever believes in him may have eternal life."

—John 3:1-15

On a children's TV program, the announcer asked a little boy what he wanted to do when he grew up. "I want to be an animal trainer," the child said loudly and clearly into the mike. "And I'll have lots of wild lions and tigers and leopards," he continued boldly. "And then I'll walk into the cage . . . . " Here, he hesitated for a second, and then added softly, "but, of course, I'll have my granddaddy with me."

Granddaddies and grandmothers are special. Ask any boy or girl. Grandsons and granddaughters are special. Ask any grandparent. Someone has said that one of life's mysteries is how the idiot that married our daughter can end up being the father of the smartest grandchildren in the whole world.

Grandchildren are special. God is special too, but God has no grandchildren. God has only children. Every generation and every individual must embrace the faith for themselves. *That's What the Man Said:* "Unless one is born anew he cannot see the kingdom of God." Only the twice-born will get to heaven. ◇ 1.

William Gibson in his autobiographical *Mass for the Dead* relates how after his mother's death he yearned for the faith that had strengthened her during her remarkable life, the faith that had upheld her during her courageous dying. So he took his mother's gold-rimmed glasses and faded and well-worn prayer book and sat in her favorite chair. He opened the prayer book because he wanted to hear what she had heard. He put on her glasses because he wanted to see what she had seen. He sat in her place of prayer and devotion because he wanted to feel what she had felt, to experience what had so deeply centered and empowered her. But nothing happened. It did not work.

It never does! We cannot claim another person's faith for our own. The example and contagion of commitment in other persons may inspire and nurture us, but we cannot substitute their commitment for our own. We can pattern our faith journey after someone else's, but no one can make that journey for us.

I doubt if anything Jesus ever said was more important than

this: "You must be born again."   ◇ **2.**   This is the hingepin of the Christian faith, and we could not give attention to what Jesus said without listening to this word. Let's listen to Jesus by asking three simple questions:

1. What is the new birth?
2. Who needs the new birth?
3. How are we born again?

First, what is the new birth? We all need to know who we are and where we came from. A little boy came in from school one day and asked his mother, "Where did I come from?" The startled mother drew her thoughts together and decided that it was time to face the issue squarely. "Ask your father when he comes home from work." When Dad arrived, the little boy said, "I've been talking with my school friends, and I wonder if you would tell me where I came from."

The father took a deep breath and proceeded to tell him about the birds and the bees. The boy's eager eyes got larger and larger. When his dad had finished, the lad jumped up and said, "Thanks, Dad. That was great! My friend Johnny, he's just from New Jersey."

We all need to know where we came from. So in response to the question "What is the new birth?" let's begin with an obvious assertion: "If you're going to grow up, you must first be born." Jesus made it clear to Nicodemus that there are two kinds of life, biological and spiritual. For either life there must be a beginning. There can be no life without birth.

So Jesus is saying that whatever is true of the physical is also true of the spiritual. You must be born into the spiritual life. Jesus uses the words flesh and spirit to talk about this: "That which is born of the flesh is flesh; that which is born of the Spirit is spirit."

Whatever else that means, and it means far more than we can fathom, much less explain in one brief study, it means that we are brought into a parent-child relationship with God.

Our relationship with God has been broken by our sin, broken beyond the possibility of human repair. The gospel is that God, through Jesus Christ, repairs what we have destroyed. And what we have destroyed by our sin is our relationship with God.

The universal picture of this broken relationship is Adam and Eve in their home, the Garden of Eden. Their relationship with God was intimate and unbroken. But by deliberate choice, by their sinful disobedience to God, Adam and Eve broke that relationship. One of the saddest pictures in all the Bible is the story at the close of Genesis 3, where God expelled Adam and Eve from the garden. The Revised Standard Version says that God drove them out. John Steinbeck picked up that image in the title of his book *East of Eden*. Instead of being residents in the garden, in ongoing intimate relationship with God in that paradise which God had prepared for

◇ **2.**
Many are suspicious of the term *born again*. Before reading further, write a couple of paragraphs expressing your honest feelings about these words.

them, the dwelling place of Adam and Eve was now "East of Eden," outside the Garden, outside the relationship with God.

And that's our story because of our sin. So the new birth is a birth to God. It is having the relationship with God, which was broken by sin, restored by grace, that is, by the loving acceptance of God through Jesus Christ.

In his Gospel, Matthew reports Jesus saying in another setting with other words the same thing he said to Nicodemus: "Except ye be converted and become as little children, ye shall not enter the kingdom of heaven" (8:3, KJV).

The image is that of becoming a child in relation to our Parent-God. And notice too that Matthew ties the word *converted* to the image of becoming like a child. That's what the new birth means. It means being converted, and being converted means becoming like a little child. The Old Testament Hebrew word is *shubh,* and it occurs almost 1,200 times. It means basically to turn or return. If you're going in one direction, it means to turn around. It means turning from sin and self, turning toward God and faith.

We have an English word, *metamorphosis,* which comes from the Greek words, *meta,* meaning "to change," and *morphe,* meaning "form." Clarence Jordan explains the process. "A little caterpillar will crawl along in the dirt and the leaves, and finally the great forces of nature—the warm weather, flowers and all—begin to work changes and he climbs up on a stem and gets real still and then something great begins to happen. He begins to split open his skin and out of that little caterpillar emerges a fragile, beautiful monarch butterfly" (Jordan, p. 38).

Jesus says that's what must happen to us in order to live in the kingdom. But "that little caterpillar can't reach down and get the nectar out of the flower. He can't even get up to the flower. He's got to have wings. He's got to have a different nose. He's got to have a different form. And Jesus is saying, 'I'm presenting you with a new order, and you've got to have the equipment to enter into it.' So the revolution begins with a call to be a certain kind of person" (Jordan, p. 39).

It must be so with us—we must *meta-morphe.* Whatever else the gospel of Jesus Christ means, it means that we humans can change, that we need to change, and that we *must* change. We must be re-born from above.

That's what the new birth means. We are born anew of the Spirit. We are brought into a Parent-child relationship with God.

◇ **3.**

Now the second question: Who needs the new birth? I think we can find our answer rather easily by looking at Nicodemus, since he is the one to whom Jesus spoke this commanding call to the soul.

Do you know who Nicodemus was? He was a ruler of the Jews, a man of position and power. He was an aristocrat, an

◇ **3.**
Describe any experiences you have had when you felt "East of Eden." Get in touch with your feelings about being brought back into a Parent-child relationship with God. Write about your feelings, describing them as clearly as you can.

educated man, a scholar. We can assume that he was now an older man, old in honor and old in years. In a sentence, Nicodemus was cultured, refined, decent, and religious. Let's look at him in our imagination as he goes through the night and knocks on the door where Jesus is staying. Jesus answers that knock, and Nicodemus stands face to face with the Savior of the world.

There were many things in the heart of this white-haired teacher that he wanted to ask Jesus. There was much that he wanted to say. He begins with the one big fact of which he is sure. "We know," he says, "that thou art a teacher come from God." Here is one who knows the mind and heart of God. And before Nicodemus can tell Him what the matter is, Jesus has answered his question, not the question of his lips, but the question of his heart.

What did He say to this man who had dared to come to Him in the night? He did not say to him, "Nicodemus, I know what the trouble is with you; you are not honest. Nicodemus you must quit swearing. Nicodemus you must quit Sabbath-breaking. You must quit breaking your marriage vows. You must stop yielding to the lusts of the flesh. No, He did not say that to this master in Israel. Had he done so, Nicodemus would have blazed upon Him, for he was guilty of none of these things. He was a clean man, a moral man, a religious man.

But what Jesus did say was this: "You must be born again." He said, "I know what is the matter. You have been trying to find peace and rest and joy and salvation by doctoring the outside of life. You have found that your well is poisonous and you have tried to remedy it by painting the well curb. You have found that the clock of life does not keep good time and you have spent endless care polishing the hands. You have found the fountain of the heart sending forth a bitter stream and you have tried to remedy it by pulling up a few weeds that grew round about it. Nicodemus, you must be put right at heart. That is first. That is fundamental."

So Jesus declared to this pious and earnest and honest man, the one supreme and universal necessity, and that is the necessity of a New Birth." (Clovis G. Chappell, pp. 54-55)

So that's the bottom linc, isn't it? Who needs the new birth? Every one of us. You see, Jesus didn't say this to an outcast. He didn't say it to one who had wasted his substance with riotous living. He said it to one of the most cultured and refined and decent and religious men of his day.

Who needs the new birth? I need the new birth. You need the new birth. Any one of us who has not yet come back from our "East of Eden" sojourn away from God—we need the new birth. I think of the parable of the prodigal son here. The young man who had spurned his father's love by wandering into the far country and spending his inheritance in riotous living came to himself and decided to go home, to return to the father who loved him.

But the prodigal isn't the only person in the story. There was the elder brother who stayed home but was still outside the father's love. In fact, he would not even enter into the joy and celebration of receiving his brother back into the household.

So we can be "East of Eden" in a lot of different ways. We may fall into the category of the father's son who wandered far from home and entered into a life of debauchery and shame. Or we may be like the elder brother, living an upright and decent life, but still outside the father's love. The prodigal brother in the far country and the prodigal brother at home, both needing the new birth, because both are outside the father's love and away from their true home.

A character in one of Flannery O'Connor's short stories asked the question, "Have you ever looked inside yourself and seen what you are not?" Well, have you?

Have you ever looked inside yourself and seen what you are not? That's sin—denying or neglecting who God is calling us to be.

• Sin is falling short of the glory of God.
• Sin is searching for self-glory and security in ourselves.
• Sin is living the unexamined life to the point that we convince ourselves we have no sin.
• Sin is ordering our lives as though we were not dependent upon God.
• Sin is convincing ourselves that we are good when the only goodness we know is our pride-producing performance that receives the acclaim of the world.   ◇ **4.**

Can we find ourselves anywhere in that picture? Who needs the new birth? Any one of us who has not come back from our "East of Eden" sojourn away from God, any one of us who is still trying to make it on our own good works, any one of us who has not yet accepted the free forgiveness of sin by God's grace.

Now the third question: How are we born again?

I have some reservations about listing specific responses we must make to receive the gospel. I am aware of what Jesus said to Nicodemus when he asked the question, "How can one be born again?"

"The wind blows where it wills, and you hear the sound of it, but you do not know from whence it comes or whither it goes; so it is with every one who is born of the Spirit."

A story is told that Beethoven once played his latest sonata for a friend. The music filled the room. As the last note lingered, the friend asked Beethoven, "What does it mean?"

Beethoven's only answer was to return to the piano and play the entire sonata again. Finished, he said to his friend, "That is what it means." Of course! How difficult it is to talk about "how" we are born again.

Let us acknowledge right off that no set formula is the answer to our new birth in Christ; the Spirit gives that birth. Even so, there is a response that we can make in order for the Spirit to work.

◇ **4.**

Do any of these definitions of sin fit at least in part where you may be now? Put a check at the beginning of two of the definitions most applicable.

First, we must repent; that is, we must be genuinely sorry for our sin, for our sojourn "East of Eden" away from God. We must genuinely desire to turn from our sins and our own efforts at saving ourselves.

Second, we must admit our need for Christ and accept his forgiveness. His forgiveness is offered; we must accept it.

Third, we invite Jesus to come into our lives, and we make the willful decision that we will accept him as our Savior and we will follow him as our Lord.

In all of this, we must remember who Jesus is and what Jesus has come to do for us and for everyone, that is, to save us, to give us the new birth. It helps us sometimes to remember that dramatic work in others. John said, "For God so loved the world that he gave his only Son that whoever believes in him should not perish but have eternal life" (3:16). We don't think much about people perishing, but in some of the forgotten corners of the world the people know that life on earth is, indeed fragile. Go to India, for instance, if you doubt that human beings can perish here on earth.

While on a tour of mission stations around the world, [Bishop F. McDowell] came to a village of India.

There one night he met with forty believing men. Knowing that they all had been outcasts, he decided to test their understanding of our religion. Hence the bishop asked:

"Brothers, who is Jesus Christ?"

Instantly forty hands went up. Then the Bishop singled out a man who did not look bright. At once the native Christian arose, bowed, and testified.

"Sir, I know that Jesus Christ is the Son of God and the Saviour of the world because he loved me and gave himself for me, and for all of us here, when no one else would touch the hem of our garments. If he looked on us in mercy, and then died to make us free, he must love everybody, he must be the Son of God. Only the good God would do what Christ has done for us outcasts."

When the Bishop came home and told us Ministers what he had heard, there shone from his eyes the glint of unshed tears. After his recital of the facts, he concluded: "It was worth going round the world more than once to hear those humble native Christians bearing witness to the Grace of Jesus Christ." "Whosoever believeth in Him should not perish, but have everlasting life." (Blackwood, pp. 96-97)

That's what we have to keep in mind, that this is who Christ is: the One who wants to give new birth.

Nothing pictures this more clearly than the parable of the prodigal son. The central truth to which I refer above is this: *When the prodigal returned home, his father accepted him as though he had never been away.* It will be so with any one of us.

You must be born again. *That's What the Man Said.* In response to his word, we simply turn to him and accept his grace

◇ **5.**
What changes in my habits, attitudes, and behavior are called for by my study of this word of Jesus?

and let the Spirit blow where it will to refresh our spirits, to give us life.

No matter how far we may have gone into the far country, the Father's home is just around the corner. Just take that "right turn," and you'll be there. For God's love is greater than your sin. God's willingness to receive us back home has no strings attached, except that we turn around (repent), come on home, and receive God's love and forgiveness. ◇ **5.**

John 3:16 follows the scripture lesson we have been looking at with this word: "For God so loved the world that he gave his only Son, that whoever believes in him should not perish but have eternal life." Make this personal. Insert your name in the blank and carry the verse with you as an ongoing affirmation.

For God so loved ——————,that he gave his only Son, that ——————, believing in him, should not perish but have eternal life.

CHAPTER ◇ 4

For God's Sake,
Be As Christian As You Are!

A young couple was in love. They had courted a long time and planned to get married. They set the date and began making all their wedding arrangements. Everything was happy and exciting, and then all of a sudden the young woman broke the engagement, saying that she was madly in love with someone else.

After eight months had passed, she wrote her former fiance this letter.

Dear Tommy,

Can you ever forgive me? No words can express how badly I feel, how terribly unhappy I've been since breaking our engagement. I can't eat. I can't sleep. I can't do anything without thinking of you. Please take me back, Tommy. Please. No one could ever take your place in my heart. I love you! I love you! I love you!

The letter was signed, "Forever, Marie." Then at the bottom, there was this little addition: "P.S. By the way, Tommy, congratulations on winning the Irish Sweepstakes!"

That P.S. would cause one to wonder whether Marie was being earnest in her expression of love. You wonder if there was not something dramatically hypocritical about her new attitude toward Tommy.

I don't hear it as much as I used to, but the word is still around—the word of people who rationalize their refusal to be a part of the church. "I have no use for the church; it's full of hypocrites." I've never had the nerve to respond to such a person with what I really wanted to say: "Oh, come on and join us! One more hypocrite won't hurt." ◇ **1.**

The word *hypocrite* is a Greek word which originally referred to one who wore a mask in Greek dramas. The basic idea is that of matching our true self with our pretended self. Or vice versa, matching our pretended self with our true self. Or put another way:

◇ **1.**
Write a one-sentence definition of *hypocrite*.

31

◇ **2.**

How does your definition of *hypocrite* harmonize with this statement: We need to be genuinely and inwardly what we seem?

◇ **3.**

You are the salt of the earth; but if salt has lost its taste, how shall its saltness be restored? It is no longer good for anything except to be thrown out and trodden under foot by men.

You are the light of the world. A city set on a hill cannot be hid. Nor do men light a lamp and put it under a bushel, but on a stand, and it gives light to all in the house. Let your light so shine before men, that they may see your good works and give glory to your Father who is in heaven.

—Matthew 5:13-16

We need to be genuinely and inwardly what outwardly we seem.

◇ **2.**

I have a new twist on the problem of hypocrisy. I confess that I did not originate this idea, but it's such a powerful idea that I want us to make it our own as we grapple with a very familiar word of Jesus. "Let your light so shine before men, that they may see your good works and give glory to your Father in heaven" (Matt. 5:16). *That's What the Man Said.*   ◇ **3.**

I encountered an idea about hypocrisy that was new to me from reading Harry Emerson Fosdick. On one of my study leaves I carried along three of Fosdick's old books. I hadn't looked at any of Fosdick's sermons in ten years. I came across one sermon entitled "On Seeming As Christian As You Are." It was in that sermon that I got this fresh notion about being a hypocrite. Fosdick says that hypocrisy has two faces. "You can get at it from two sides. Some people are hypocrites because they profess a Christian faith they are not living. Others are hypocrites because deep within themselves they have genuine Christianity they are not showing."

Now that's the new idea. Does it grab you as it grabbed me? We can be hypocrites by professing a Christian faith we are not living. But we can also be hypocrites by not showing to the world and saying to the world the Christian we are.

In *The Power to See It Through,* Fosdick says that "some hypocrites need to be told, be a good as you seem; other hypocrite need to be told, seem as good as you are." After giving that insight Fosdick used an illustration to make his point.

A generation ago, the principal of one of our leading boys' schools addressed a group of freshmen entering Harvard and, in effect, said this: "If I were speaking on any other campus, I probably would not say what I am going to say to you. But I know Harvard. I am a Harvard man myself and I understand the sophisticated atmosphere into which you freshmen now are venturing, so that while on any other campus I might say to you, be as religious as you seem, I say to you, seem as religious as you are. (Fosdick, *The Power to See it Through,* p. 162)

So you see where I get the title for this chapter: For God's Sake, Be As Christian As You Are! I believe that's what Jesus was saying—be as Christian as you are: "Let your light so shine before men, that they may see your good works and give glory to your Father who is in heaven." *That's What the Man Said,* and that's what I want us to consider in this chapter.

Let's press this issue by making the plea which is in the chapter title: *Be as Christian as you are.* I hope the unusual nature of that expression will be enough to cause you to remember the plea: Be as Christian as you are. Fosdick helps us think clearly about the issue.

Two things the Master could not endure: cruelty and sham. We are familiar with those passages where he assailed sham, all the way from mild ones like, "Sound not a trumpet before thee, as the hypocrites do in the synagogues and in the streets, that they may have glory of men," to terrible ones like, "whited sepulchres, which outwardly appear beautiful, but inwardly are full of dead men's bones, and of all uncleanness."

So, someone says, "that is what hypocrisy meant to Jesus— trying to appear better than we are." Surely! But listen to the other side of the matter. What about appearing worse than we are? "Neither do men light a candle, and put it under a bushel, but on a candlestick; and it giveth light unto all that are in the house. Let your light so shine before men that they may see . . . ." [*That's What the Man Said*] So! to have light and keep it dark, to have some radiance in you, though it be but the slender flame of the candle, and hide it, to refuse to set it out where the generation that so desperately needs it can get its full effect—that is hypocrisy too. That also is failure to square what we seem to be with what we are. (Fosdick, *The Power to See It through* p. 163) ◇ **4.**

Fosdick is asking an important question. If it is hypocritical to pretend to be *better* than we are by the same token, aren't we hypocritical when we appear to be *worse* than we are?

We need to square what we seem to be with what we are. *That's What the Man Said:* "Don't light a lamp and put it under a bushel, but let your light shine before men" (AP). Seem as Christian as you are.

Let's get to the overall theme of what Jesus is saying. *No Christian walks incognito.*

Now, I know that most of us wear masks on occasion and we often try to disguise ourselves. I remember having dinner at the Peabody Hotel in Memphis one Halloween night. It followed the celebration of the wedding of our unofficially adopted son, Fred Davis. Our table was at a window looking out on a part of the lobby and on one of the large corridors of the hotel. The dinner was delicious, but the parade through the corridor was a feast of hilarity. During dinner, we saw Presidents Nixon and Reagan, Tarzan and Jane, live mummies, and the devil with a long tail and a pitchfork. Then there were three people in a shower and there was a fire hydrant. That's right—a live fire hydrant walked by.

It was a dramatic reminder of the fact that not only on Halloween but throughout life we often try to disguise ourselves. We try to be who we are not. Some of us pretend to be better than we are, but many of us act as if we were a lot worse than we really are. But the truth is that no Christian walks incognito. If you are a Christian, you cannot forever hide the fact that you are. ◇ **5.**

If we are living faithfully, keeping our promises with quiet determination and living out truth, other persons will know it. If we are patient and constant with friends and strangers, and if we are willing to help, to take risks, and love the unlovely, such goodness and affirmation cannot be kept incognito. To live as a Christian is to love—and it shows if we

◇ **4.**
Recall and describe an experience within the past two months when you were a hypocrite because you didn't *seem as Christian as you are*.

◇ **5.**
Think about a person to whom you have been an effective witness. What was it about your witness that made it effective? Make same notes here.

◇ **6.**

The following are descriptions of three kinds of people. Do you know someone who fits each category? Think about your reasons for placing a person in one of these categories:

• people who are long on good deeds, but short on good words;

———————————————————
name of person(s)

• people who are long on good words, but short on good deeds;

———————————————————
name of person(s)

• people who say a lot with their words and with their deeds.

———————————————————
name of person(s)

Which kind of person are you? Why did you place yourself in that category?

◇ **7.**

Describe an experience when someone shined his or her light *at* you rather than *before* you. Can you remember doing that to someone?

◇ **8.**

List the first persons who come to your mind when I say, "Name three Christians in your community." Are any of these persons showy? How do they let their faith show?

———————————————————

———————————————————

———————————————————

are following Christ with genuine commitment. We will not have to waste much time telling anyone, or being defensive about our spirituality; they will know. It will be revealed in the joy and kindness, the respect we show other persons and the reverence for life we live out. Persons meeting us will see it in our faces. Inner radiance, joy, and peace cannot be masked. Warmth and receptivity, caring and openness become a light in our eyes, a smile, a look of welcome and acceptance.

Moreover, at summit moments our faces glow, as did Jesus' face on the Mount of Transfiguration . . . . To live is to love—and it shows in our faces. (Shelby, January 16, 1977)

No Christian walks incognito.   ◇ **6.**

Let's move this one step further along into very practical instructions for our daily living. This call of Jesus to be as Christian as we are means at least two things. One, we are to let our lights shine before others—not at them.

Get that! We are to let our light shine before others, *not at them.*

Did you ever have someone try to help you with a flashlight through a dark place where the footing was uncertain? If you have, then you have shared my experience of having the person shine the flashlight not on the precarious path but directly in your eyes! That kind of help does not bless you; it blinds you. Yet, how frequently virtue is flaunted in other people's faces in just such a self-defeating fashion.   ◇ **7.**

Do you recall that old story of the contest between the wind and the sun to see which one could get a topcoat off a man faster? To demonstrate his prowess, the wind tried to strip the coat off the man as he walked across the field. At the wind's first blast, the man pulled the coat ever more tightly about him. Frustrated, the wind blew harder. In turn, the man turned up his collar. Finally, as the wind shrieked and howled, the man buttoned his coat clear up around his chin. The wind gave up, and the sun took a turn. The sun beamed benignly on the man. It gently wrapped him in its warmth until the man quite voluntarily unbuttoned his coat, spread it open, and finally took it off.

Bishop Melvin Wheatley, reflecting on this story in a sermon, said, "I suspect parents and preachers, teachers, and politicians, singers and salesmen—all of us—have much to learn from the method of the sun. . . . For the sun respected the personal integrity of the man whom it was trying to influence. Whereas the wind blustered, 'I'll get that coat off of you if I have to rip it off a thread at a time'; the sun understood that the coat would, could and should come off only when and as the man himself removed it."

That makes the point doesn't it? We are to let our lights shine before others, not *at* them.

Closely akin to this is a second practical instruction expressed a bit differently: Our Christian faith must show but not be showy.   ◇ **8.**

A questionnaire was circulated among the children in a New Jersey elementary school. The teachers were trying to discover which pupils needed special attention to develop their social attitudes. One question was, "Which student in this class brags the least about herself?" One twelve-year-old girl put down her own name!

We laugh at that, but it's an uncomfortable laugh if we really examine our lives. We know that we can be so proud of our humility that we never suspect that we are not humble. We can be so confident in our self-sufficiency that we are not even aware of our inadequacies. Though we all abhor false humility, when we look at ourselves we might find that we are showy with our Christian faith—rather than humble enough to simply let our Christian faith show.

We have to be careful how we witness and how we live as Christians.   ◇ **9.**

Never, never must we present an air of spiritual superiority. Our Christian witness is never effective if there is any hint of self-righteousness in it—if our virtue can be reduced to priggishness.

> Good works done in order to be seen . . . will finally sour. We soon grow weary with such well-doing to impress, especially when things don't come out as planned and we are not properly recognized or commended. To live is to love—and it shows, but it is never showy. "When you give," Jesus said, "do not let your left hand know what your right hand is doing, so that you may give in secret, and your Father who sees in secret will reward you openly." (Shelby, January 16, 1977)

In his autobiographical work, *Adventures in Two Worlds,* the doctor–novelist, A. J. Cronin, illustrates this same point when he writes:

> I have told you of Olwen Davies, the middle-aged nurse who for more than twenty years, with fortitude and patience, calmness and cheerfulness, served the people of [a Welsh village.] This unconscious selflessness, which above all seemed the key-note of her character, was so poorly rewarded it worried me. Although she was much beloved by the people, her salary was inadequate. And late one night, after a particular strenuous case, I ventured to protest to her as we drank a cup of tea together."
> "Nurse," I said, "why don't you make them pay you more? It's ridiculous that you should work for so little." She raised her eyebrows a little. But she smiled. "I have enough to get along."
> "No, really," I protested, "You ought to have an extra pound a week at least. God knows you are worth it . . . " There was a pause. Her smile remained but her gaze held a gravity, and intensity which startled me. "Doctor," she said, "If God knows I'm worth it, that's all that matters to me." (Cronin, p. 32)

"Let your light shine." *That's What the Man Said.* He's

◇ **9.**
Name two persons with whom you have failed as a witness.

_____

_____

In two or three sentences tell why you think you failed.

◇ **10.**
State in your own words the basic principles involved in this saying of Jesus: "Let your light so shine before men, that they may see your good works and give glory to your Father who is in heaven."

reminding us that we can't be Christian incognito. He's calling for a faith that shines *before*, not *at*, people; a faith that shows but is not showy.

So I urge you—for God's sake and for the sake of the world, *be as Christian as you are.*   ◇ **10.**

What changes in your attitudes, habits, and/or lifestyle are called for if you take Jesus seriously?

CHAPTER ◇ 5

Never Apologize for Being Human

When the death of President Calvin Coolidge was made public, someone quipped, "How can they tell?"

How foreign that lifelessness to the vibrant dynamic power Jesus offers! Listen to him: "Truly, truly, I say to you, he who believes in me will also do the works that I do; and greater works than these will he do, because I go to the Father" (John 14:12). *That's What the Man Said.* ◇ **1.**

What a breathtaking promise! On the surface of it, it seems incredible. If this is even remotely possible, then mustn't we admit that we have never taken Jesus seriously? The least we have to confess is that we have certainly been satisfied with far less than he has in mind for us as his followers.

I think of one of Charles Schulz's *Peanuts* cartoons. Snoopy (the dog) says that Woodstock (the bird) would some day be a great eagle. Then in the next frame he says that Woodstock will soar "thousands of feet" high.

Then Woodstock takes off into the air. As Snoopy looks on, he sees Woodstock upside-down and whirling around crazily. So he has second thoughts. In the next frame Snoopy reconsiders and concludes that maybe "hundreds of feet" is more accurate.

But just then, Woodstock falls to the ground, looking dazed, and Snoopy has to conclude that Woodstock may be "one of those eagles who just walks around."

Isn't it amazing how quickly we settle for less than is promised and is possible?

S. R. Crockett in his preface to John Galt's *Annals of the Parish* tells us that in his beloved countryside of Scotland there is a churchyard in which lie buried whole generations of a family. On each of the tombstones there is cut the name, and then this, as the summing up of their endeavors and achievements: "They kept shop in Wigtown—and that's all."

We at least smile at that—"They kept shop . . . and that's all." Probably good people, all of them. But greater works than Christ? What might be written on our tombstones? Good

◇ **1.**
"Truly, truly I say to you, he who believes in me will also do the works that I do; and greater works than these will he do, because I go to the Father. Whatever you ask in my name, I will do it, that the Father may be glorified in the Son; if you ask anything in my name, I will do it."
—John 14:12-14

◇ **2.**

Read the scripture on the previous page *aloud*. Silently reflect on its meaning, then write down five different words that capture your feelings and thoughts about it.

◇ **3.**

When was the last time you made this response, "I'm only human," as a way of saying no to something someone wanted you to do or in response to some difficult situation you were struggling with, or to explain some failure in your life, or to back away from some urging you were feeling? Recall and describe that experience here.

◇ **4.**

When you use the phrase "I am only human," do you find yourself emphasizing the word *only*?

Are you putting down being human?

Are you putting yourself down?

Does to speak in that fashion suggest that humans are relegated to very low status in the ultimate scheme of things?

folks? loved their family? kind? gentle? good citizens? giving? But greater works than Christ?

Is this an idle word of Jesus, a word that has no connection with the reality of things? "Even if we believe in Christ and seek to serve him, it looks as if most of us can do but little. We're plain and ordinary folk with one talent, if that; our sphere is cramped and limited; do it as thoroughly as we may, our work seems to make little difference; we fall out in the end and nothing stops; things just go on; someone else fills our office; and in a little while, we are never missed or so much as remembered . . ." (Gossip, p. 705).

So what have we here in this word of Jesus? "Greater works than these will [you] do, because I go to the Father."

That's What the Man Said—the One who came to save the world. The One who healed and forgave and loved and washed his disciples' feet. The One who calmed the storm and took little children on his lap and blessed them. The One who ate with sinners and flung his life in the teeth of the raw and rampant prejudice of his day by conversing with the Samaritan woman. The One who finished all the work God gave him to do and is now crowned with glory and honor. *That's What the Man Said*, "Greater works than these will [you] do, because I go to the Father." ◇ **2.**

Well, it is an incredible word—and not too many of us have waited long in openness and listened to it. It is for another time and place and for other persons than the likes of us, we may think. But let's at least give attention to the word. Let's at least, in our minds, flirt with what it might mean, what it *could* mean. Maybe our flirtation will become a courtship, and we will become open to the almost limitless power for living Christ is offering.

Let's seek to appropriate the message of this word under the rubric *Never apologize for being human.* ◇ **3.**

Isn't that our common response? "I'm only human, you know." When some great possibility opens, when some challenge is thrust upon us, when the invitation comes to break step with the crowd, we easily respond, as though we were expressing good reason, "I'm only human."

We're still using *being human* as a cop-out. Even after the "human potential" revolution and the humanistic psychology movement with convincing prophets like Abraham Maslow. Even after the thousands of books that have been written on the amazing untapped power that belongs to all of us, we still use being human as a cop-out. Does it seem as ironical and as paradoxical to you as it does to me? We are come-of-age people. We pride ourselves in our enlightenment and ingenuity as human beings. In a supposedly humanistic age when many people have sloughed off religion and pinned their hopes on human achievement, these same people protest "but I'm only human!" ◇ **4.**

We keep doing it—apologizing for being human. I want to register three affirmations to bolster my admonition, "Never apologize for being human." In approaching it this way, we might be able to begin to appropriate what Jesus said: "Greater works than these will [you] do, because I go to the Father."

Let's begin with a truth which you have heard so often and in so many different settings that your mind may be dull to it. It's a truth, no matter how it might have been used to undergird some weak, selfish, or perverted system. *You are more than you think you are!* I believe that's a part of what Jesus is saying to us.

I read recently of an elderly bachelor and a never-married woman who started going together. Each had lived alone for many years. Gradually, the old gentleman recognized a real attachment for the woman but was shy and afraid to tell her his feelings. Finally, he mustered up the courage to say, "Let's get married!" Surprised, she threw up her hands and shouted, "It's wonderful to think about, but who in the world would have us?"

It's easy to sink into that kind of not-worth-much-self-understanding. When I'm blue and am down on myself, when depression threatens to turn the sky of my life into dark clouds of gloom, when I sense that I'm becoming too preoccupied with failure, I try to remember Psalm 8. Do you remember it?

> When I look at thy heavens, the work of thy fingers, the moon and the stars which thou hast established; what is man that thou art mindful of him, and the son of man that thou dost care for him? Yet thou has made him little less than God [some translations have it "a little lower than the angels"], and dost crown him with glory and honor.
>
> —Psalm 8:3-5

If I can put this word of the psalmist together with Jesus' teaching, "Greater works than these will [you] do because I go to the Father," then I can know that I am more than I think I am. The psalmist goes on to say, "Thou hast given him dominion over the works of thy hands; thou hast put all things under his feet" (v. 6). Not unlike what Jesus said: "Greater works than these will he do, because I go to the Father."

So nail it down: You are more than you think you are. Robert Seymour suggests that the phrase "I'm only human" represents a secularization of a basic theological truth.

> It is a way of acknowledging that we are not God, that we are the creature and not the Creator, of reminding ourselves and others of our status in the scheme of things, and of admitting that you and I are not altogether in charge here; God is.
>
> .   .   .   .
>
> Members of an earlier generation were more ready to admit this aspect of our humanity than we are, and so in some situations to which we respond with twinges of guilt, we say instead, "Well, I'm only human." It is a softer, more comfortable statement of fact, conveying very little—if any—awareness of judgment. Instead of crying out,

◇ **5.**
Spend some time reflecting on Robert Seymour's remarks.

"O, Lord, be merciful to me a sinner," we complain: "God, I'm only human. What did you expect?" (Seymour, p. 28)   ◇ **5.**

Either secular meaning of that expression "I'm only human" is limited. It certainly doesn't help us in our relationship to God as far as our sin is concerned to pass it off simply as the result of being human. And to acknowledge that we are creature and God is Creator is well and good. This should always be a part of our awareness—being human means being limited. Even so, we are more than we think we are.

Now a second truth: *There is something you can be, but will never be, apart from Jesus Christ.* Listen to what Jesus said: "Greater works than these will [you] do, because I go to the Father." There is something you can be, but will never be, apart from Jesus Christ.

In 1985, after the disastrous earthquake that hit Mexico City, the *Los Angeles Times* reported a beautiful story that took place in the streets of its city. A little Japanese-American boy decided that he would like to do something to help the earthquake victims. When he heard that the damages had gone into the millions of dollars, he decided that he would like to raise one million dollars himself to send to those victims. He started going door to door in Los Angeles selling postcards for twenty-five cents. When he came to one house and presented his cause, the man there asked him how much he hoped to raise. Without even hesitating, the little boy said, "One million dollars!"

"One million dollars!" exclaimed the man. "That's a lot of money. Do you expect to raise it all by yourself?" I like the little boy's answer: "Oh, sir, there's another little boy helping me!"

What does that say to you and me? Commitment and expectation of that sort enable us to tackle the impossible. Add that to the divine factor—the *plus* of Christ's power, and you have the story of countless millions of persons who have proven what Jesus said was true: "Greater works than these will [you] do."

In his own day, Christ made only a passing impression on his little homeland and almost none on the world beyond it. Yet his followers have won large numbers for him, far more than he ever gained himself. People by the millions have been healed in his name in lands that would never have heard his name, much less been healed, had not missionary doctors and nurses gone to those far-flung corners of the earth with the healing love of Jesus Christ. And little children, by the tens of thousands, are being kept from starvation today by people who are doing his works. It is not important to list the mighty works or name the names of people who have done those works. That list would almost be without end. What is important is that those who have done those works all say that it was not they who did it but, as Arthur John Gossip relates in the *Interpreter's Bible,* "that the inspiration, the power, the endurance that made it possible all came from Jesus Christ; that if he had passed out of being on Calvary, if he had not gone to his Father, had not remembered them, and planned for them, and stood by them, and supplied all their need, all the achievements that men credit to them would have been utterly impossible."

Jesus said to his followers in our scripture lesson, and he says to us:

Things are not collapsing, . . . But together, you and I will see this through. And remember there are two of us; that you will never be sent out or left alone; always it will be you—and I; and together what can we not accomplish—you and I? The grace you saw for yourselves to be so effective in my hands is not withdrawn from the world. It lies at your disposal. Draw on it; draw on me; ask of me; lean on me; look to me; and there is no limit to what we can accomplish. (Gossip, p. 706)

There is something you can be but will never be apart from Jesus Christ. You don't have to think of it dramatically. Think of your day-to-day life.

Jesus can make you the loving person that you can never be without him. Jesus can make you the forgiving person that you can never be apart from him. Jesus can make you the witnessing person that you can never be apart from him. Jesus can make you the serving person that you can never be apart from him. ◇ **6.**

Out of tragic South Africa comes a poignant story of what I am saying. Alan Paton tells the story in his 1982 novel, *Ah, But Your Land Is Beautiful*. The story takes place during the Maundy Thursday service of the Holy Church of Zion. The ritual of foot-washing preceded Holy Communion. The pastor, who was black, invited Judge Oliver to come to the service to wash the feet of Martha Fortuin, a black woman who had raised and cared for the judge's children. Judge Oliver was a white man of character, willing to stand against his fellow jurists on issues where principle was involved. The judge, remembering how Martha Fortuin had often kissed the feet of his children, bent over to kiss her feet after he ritually washed them. Tears filled the eyes of other worshipers in the tiny church. The press learned of the event and publicized it widely. As a result, Judge Oliver lost the chief judgeship, which was to have been his.

A few days later the black pastor called on Judge Oliver to ask him to forgive him for being instrumental in destroying him professionally. The judge replied, "Taking part in your service on Maundy Thursday is to me more important than any chief judgeship. Think no more about it." And that is why the people of the Holy Church of Zion renamed their church in South Africa the Church of the Washing of Feet.

Like Judge Oliver, there is something we can be, but will never be, apart from Jesus Christ.

Let me register the third affirmation to bolster my admoni-

◇ **6.**
Name two limitations of your life that you would like to have changed, ways you would like to be different.

Have you ever surrendered these limitations to Christ, asked him for his power, and willingly yielded yourself to his changing power? Write a brief prayer, making that commitment now.

◇ **7.**
Write two or three sentences in response to the following questions:

What does it mean to pray in Jesus' name?

What is the connection between prayer and faith?

tion: Never apologize for being human. *Prayer is the human act that enables us to transcend the limitation of being human—to link ourselves with the power Jesus offers only humans.* Think of it. No other form of life can pray. Jesus links his amazing word, "greater works than these will you do because I go to the Father," with his equally amazing promise about prayer in verses 13 and 14: "Whatever you ask in my name, I will do it, that the Father may be glorified in the Son; if you ask anything in my name, I will do it."

Do you note that he says the same thing twice? It is obvious that he wants that to register in our minds. So try to get the full impact of what Jesus wanted to convey. Pay close attention. He didn't say, "Ask anything in my name and I will probably do it." Jesus did not say, "Ask anything in my name and I might do it." Nor did he say, "Ask, and there's a good chance that what you ask you will get." No, he was very emphatic. "Ask anything in my name and I will do it."

"But wait a minute," you say. "I'm not sure I really believe that!"

I'm with you. I know what you're talking about. Those gnawing doubts recur often in my life. It's so easy to stumble upon that promise. It's such a big, big, sweeping, extravagant, emphatic promise. It's so easy to draw back from it and to raise big questions. We've been told to ask and we have asked and have gone away empty-handed. We've been told to seek and we have sought, but nothing has come of it. We've been told to knock and we've knocked, and the door seems still to be closed. When people make a response like that about the limitation of their own prayer life and how they have been disappointed in their praying, it doesn't help to remind them that they may have been praying amiss or that they may have a naive conception of what prayer does. What does help, in all instances, is for us to be reminded that the promise Jesus gives us here is not unconditional. Rather, this promise is explicitly and strictly limited. It is only what we ask for in Christ's name, only what we pray for his sake that he promises to give us.

So we can confidently count on receiving what we ask *only* if what we ask will advance God's cause and bring God glory. *That's What the Man Said*, "Whatever you ask *in my name*, I will do it, *that the Father may be glorified* in the Son." So we pray in Christ's name and for what will give God glory.

Notice another connection and condition: the connection between faith and prayer. Look precisely at what Jesus said: "He who believes in me will also do the works that I do" (v. 12)—that's an underscoring of faith. "Whatever you ask in my name I will do it" (v. 13)—that's an underscoring of prayer. The two are inseparably linked. ◇ **7.**

Our power depends on our prayer, and our prayer depends upon our faith. If we as individuals, as well as our Christian community, are impotent, or all but impotent, we should not have any difficulty understanding why. We are not in connection with the source of power. We've shut off the tap. We lack faith, and our power is weakness.

You remember that question of the disciples, "Why could we not cast him out?" They were talking about the fact that Jesus had cast out demons that they were impotent to deal with. They should not have been perplexed. "Why could we not cast him out?" Jesus responds. Because you do not believe that I, working in you, can cast him out. That is why; it is the only why.

> When they came to the crowd, a man came up to him and kneeling before him said, "Lord, have mercy on my son, for he is epileptic and he suffers terribly; for often he falls into the fire, and often into the water. And I brought him to your disciples, and they could not heal him." And Jesus answered, "O, faithless and perverse generation, how long am I to be with you? How long am I to bear with you? Bring him here to me." And Jesus rebuked him, and the demon came out of him, and the boy was cured instantly. Then the disciples came to Jesus privately and said, "Why could we not cast it out?" He said to them, "Because of your little faith. For truly, I say to you, if you have faith as a grain of mustard seed, you will say to this mountain, 'Move from here to there, to yonder place,' and it will move; and nothing will be impossible to you."
>
> —Matthew 17:14-21

The secret of the Christian's weakness is the weakness of the Christian's faith. ◇ **8.**

And that brings us to another connection I want to make about prayer, faith, and *the greater work that we can do*. That connection is in the scripture which follows the scripture we are looking at.

> If you love me, you will keep my commandments. And I will pray the Father, and he will give you another Counselor, to be with you for ever, even the Spirit of truth, whom the world cannot receive, because it neither sees him nor knows him; you know him, for he dwells with you, and will be in you.
>
> —John 14:15-17

Here is Jesus' promise of the Holy Spirit—the promise of his Indwelling Presence. In the New Testament alone, the Spirit is referred to nearly three hundred times, and the one word with which the Spirit is constantly associated is *power*. If Christ is with us, and he has given his word that he is, then no wonder we don't ever need to apologize for being human. We can believe that greater works than Jesus did when he was in the flesh can be done now because Jesus has been released from the flesh and indwells all of us who receive him by faith.

Do you get the picture? During his earthly life Jesus laid hands on a few sick folks and healed them. He spoke to people,

◇ **8.**
Spend a few minutes in prayer, reflecting on this assertion: "The secret of the Christian's weakness is the weakness of the Christian's faith."
How is this demonstrated in your life? Write a brief paragraph here.

◇ **9.**

Name here one thing that you would like to do, but you've never attempted because of fear of failure.

Is this something you believe Christ wants you to do?

If so, pray for his power and guidance and begin now to seek to do it.

Name two or three things you think your church needs to do in ministry but has not sought to do because it feels the resources to perform the ministries are not available.

Name here some friends in the church with whom you can share your thoughts.

In the next few days, tell your friends about this and invite them to begin to pray with you that the church will tackle these goals.

bidding them to follow him, and some of them did. There were 120 disciples at Jerusalem and 500 in Galilee when he died. That was what Christ had been able to do. But think about it now! Because Christ indwells us, we—as millions of Christians before us have been—can be the leaven of the kingdom in our own sphere here, there, yonder, all over the world, as the kingdoms of the earth are impacted by the kingdom of Christ. "Greater works than these will you do." ◇ **9.**

That's What the Man Said, so never apologize for being human. Only humans can pray, and anything you ask in Jesus' name that is for the sake of the kingdom, for the Glory of God, Jesus will give. Our prayers are linked with our faith, and our faith is linked with the spirit of the Indwelling Christ. The greater work we do then is the work of Christ, who has been set free from earthly limitations and exercises his mighty works through you and me.

Remember that wonderful story about the Lord asking Moses to go down to Egypt and demand of Pharaoh the release of the Hebrew slaves? "Not me, Lord," Moses replied. "I'm only human. I'm not eloquent; I'm slow of speech; nobody will listen to me." And the Lord asked, "Moses, who made your mouth? I will be with you and teach you what to say." We are never *only* human when we're related to the living God. God came to us in Jesus Christ, became human to show us clearly what the divine intention is for our human life.

Earlier, I shared Snoopy's dashed hopes about Woodstock's being a soaring eagle. I close this chapter with a Native American legend about the changeling eagle.

A brave found an eagle's egg and put it into the nest of a prairie chicken. The eaglet hatched with a brood of chicks and grew up with them. All his life, the eagle, thinking he was a prairie chicken, did what the prairie chickens did. He scratched in the dirt for seeds and insects to eat. He clucked and cackled. And he flew in a brief thrashing of wings and flurry of feathers no more than a few feet off the ground. After all, that's how prairie chickens were supposed to fly.

Years passed. The changeling eagle grew very old. One day he saw a magnificent bird far above him in the cloudless sky. Hanging with graceful majesty on the powerful wind currents, the bird soared with scarcely a beat of its strong golden wings.

"That's a beautiful bird," said the changeling eagle. "What is it?"

"That's an eagle, the chief of the birds," the neighbor clucked. "But don't give it a second thought. You could never be like him."

So the changeling eagle never gave it another thought, and it died thinking it was a prairie chicken.

Eagles—prairie chickens—Christians in name only. "Truly, truly I say to you, he who believes in me will also do the

works that I do; and greater works than these will he do, because I
go to the Father." *That's What the Man Said.*

> Is there a greater tragedy—
> To die without knowing who you are
> Or to live denying who you are?
> I urge you, never apologize for being human.
> But more crucial than that,
> Lay hold of the power that is given you by
>   the Christ who indwells you.

CHAPTER ◇ 6

What Can I Get By With?

◇ **1.**

The apostles said to the Lord, "Increase our faith!" And the Lord said, "If you had faith as a grain of mustard seed, you could say to this sycamine tree, 'Be rooted up, and be planted in the sea,' and it would obey you. Will any one of you, who has a servant plowing or keeping sheep, say to him when he has come in from the field, 'Come at once and sit down at table'? Will he not rather say to him, 'Prepare supper for me, and gird yourself and serve me, till I eat and drink; and afterward you shall eat and drink'? Does he thank the servant because he did what was commanded? So you also, when you have done all that is commanded you, say, 'We are unworthy servants; we have only done what was our duty.' "

—Luke 17:5-10

A son at college was trying to apply pressure for more money from his dad. In a letter home he wrote, "I can't understand why you call yourself a loving father when you haven't sent me a check for three weeks. What kind of love do you call that?"

The father wrote back, "That's unremitting love!"

We smile at that. Some of us may even chuckle, though not out loud, because we have been there. But who has ever defined love that way—*unremitting*? We usually think of it in completely opposite terms—total giving. We call it unconditional love. We certainly think of God that way. That's the way Jesus revealed a God who gives and gives and gives until there is nothing left to give. That's the reason this word of Jesus for our consideration in this chapter is such a shocking one. "When you have done all that is commanded you, say, 'We are unworthy servants; we have only done what was our duty' " (Luke 17:10). *That's What the Man Said.*

◇ **1.**

This is one of Jesus' least familiar sayings. It's one of his most confusing and one of his toughest. Though confusing and tough, this saying doesn't let us off the hook. One preacher, Terrence Johnson, was so frustrated with this parable and saying of Jesus as he sought to prepare a sermon on it that he ended up writing Luke a letter which became his sermon.

Dear Luke,
You're a terrific writer, and through the years I've become more appreciative of your *Gospel* (along with your second volume, *The Acts of the Apostles*). There's a wonderfully human touch to your writing, even in the midst of the mysterious. Your story of the birth of Jesus is a masterpiece; and our churches have listened to children read it for many Christmases. Your inclusion of the parable of the Good Samaritan is a literary jewel. And the resurrection appearance to the two disciples on the road to Emmaus is one of the most intriguing and touching of the post-resurrection stories.

I like your Gospel, Luke; but I'm having some *real difficulty* with your little parable about the farmer and the slave. It's not exactly a heart-warming story, nor is it a mountain-peak experience of Bible reading. How could you write something like that! Look again at how you end it, man: "When you have done all that is commanded you, say, 'We are unworthy servants; we have only done what was our duty.' " Now doesn't that sound like a real "downer!" (Johnson, p. 479)

◇ **2.**

Well, it does, doesn't it? This passage is not easy and simple to deal with, yet it offers much needed lessons to us.

Obviously—and we can't escape it—the parable Jesus tells and his harsh words of teaching are first of all words about duty. We have difficulty with the story because of the harshness of the slave system in Jesus' day. Also, our neck stiffens in anger at the churlish, calloused master who never says thank you. He must have been an unfeeling, inconsiderate man. No compassion at all. His servant had been plowing all day in the field, literally "slaving." He came in at sundown, his back aching, his whole body numb with weariness. But there is no acknowledgment of what has been done, only another duty laid upon him. He must now prepare his master's supper and wait until his master has eaten before he can sit and rest his weary muscles and renew his strength by whatever food is left.

A harsh picture of the severity of duty. It's that backdrop against which Jesus speaks to us. "So you also, when you have done all that is commanded you, say, 'We are unworthy servants; we have only done what was our duty.' " No wonder we get our backs up at such a word!

But let's get beyond our seething distaste for the inconsiderate master and speak a good word for duty. I believe that's what Jesus was doing.

Duty is not a pleasant word. We frown at it as it relates to morality. A school boy on his examination paper wrote this: "The Christian religion allows a man only one wife. The system is called 'monotony.' "

One supposes that that's one of the reasons for the failure of a good many marriages, so we've done something about it. We've done something about it by developing a so-called "new" morality. It is as though every generation thinks it can change the moral structure by majority vote.   ◇ **3.**

Duty is not a pleasant word. It's not pleasant because we've come to the place in our society when an all-too-common motto is "What is the least I can do to get by?"

The blunt truth is that we are the creators of a society where patterns of behavior, moral standards, and spiritual ideals have been undermined by negligence, cheating, corruption, lying, stealing, and immoral acts on the grounds that everybody is doing it and that any kind of worthwhile aim justifies the means.

Jesus is telling us in this harsh word that there is an "oughtness" to life. There are demands that are placed upon us

◇ **2.**
Reread the parable. Write a paragraph expressing your honest feelings and questions about the story and Jesus' concluding word.

◇ **3.**
Name three areas in modern life in which what we consider "right" or "moral duty" has changed because the feelings of most people about these issues have changed so significantly, e.g. premarital sex.

Write a paragraph about the connection between duty and morality. What determines duty? What determines morality?

◇ **4.**

Reflect for a few minutes on this question: In what sense does popular opinion determine morality and duty?

◇ **5.**

Take a reflective look at your life. What areas of involvement or what relationship tends most to lead you to self-pity? Make some notes about this.

◇ **6.**

Try to be as honest as possible. If it has been so, write a few sentences describing an involvement or accomplishment in the past few months that led to at least *faint feelings* of self-righteousness.

which allow no letting up in discipline. There is a sense in which we can never say, "Thank God, I'm finished with that. I can now rest. I deserve a break."

So duty is not a dirty four-letter word. It's a word whose meaning needs desperately to be recovered in our day.   ◇ **4.**

Let's move now to another perspective. A healthy sense of duty would save us from two debilitating sins—the sins of *self-pity* and *self-righteousness*. If we don't have a good perspective on duty, it's easy to fall into self-pity and/or self-righteousness.

Isn't it easy, parents, to fall into a slough of self-pity because of all the demands that are made of you by your children, your home, and your job? All of us are victims of self-pity. "What's the use?" we say. "The people in Washington get away with murder, the rich get richer, and the poor get poorer. Why should I keep on paying these taxes? What good is it doing?"   ◇ **5.**

We would be saved a lot of emotional energy if we could keep a right perspective on the fact that we have duties. As citizens, we have duties; as members of the church, we have duties. Performing those duties doesn't mean that we are going to receive any kind of special consideration. Therefore, what right have we to say, "I've done everything right; why should this happen to me?" or "I've done my duty, what have I done to deserve this?" We're really getting to the point of extreme self-pity when we began to think and say, "It seems the more good you do, the worse off you are."

Closely akin to self-pity is self-righteousness. A right perspective on duty might save us from self-righteousness.

Aren't we all guilty? We do what is expected of us and even more. We begin to feel good. We teach Sunday school, we sing in the choir, we serve on the evangelism work area. We work on Habitat for Humanity housing; we serve with the youth ministry of our church. We feel good about what we are doing. We even feel righteous. What right has the preacher or a committee chairman to ask me to do anything else, to add to the commitments I've already made? Then boom! We're confronted with Jesus' word: "When you have done all that is commanded you, say 'We are unworthy servants; we have only done what was our duty.' "   ◇ **6.**

Jesus may have said it even more strongly when he said, "Woe to you, scribes and Pharisees, hypocrites! For you tithe mint and dill and cummin, and have neglected the weightier matters of the law, justice and mercy and faith. These you ought to have done, without leaving the others undone" (Matt. 23:23).

Maybe this is the reason we don't like the hard saying of Jesus. It reveals our self-righteousness, and it condemns our smug attitude of ever thinking that we measure up to the kingdom's demands. Is there any way that any one of us, by any amount of effort or obedience to the will of God, can establish a claim for a reward? In *Expositions of Holy Scripture,* Alexander Maclaren rightly reminds us that for a person to call himself or herself an unprofitable servant is a blessed thing; for the Master to call us one is an awful thing.   ◇ **7.**

Do you see the difference? For God to call us an unprofitable servant is an act of judgment on God's part. But to call ourselves unprofitable servants is to judge ourselves as well we might. It is to acknowledge, as Paul said, that "none is righteous, no, not one" (Rom. 3:10), for we have all sinned and fallen short of the glory of God.

So a healthy sense of duty saves us from two debilitating sins: the sin of self-pity and the sin of self-righteousness.   ◇ **8.**

That leads to a final thought this word of Jesus calls us to pursue. Everything on the surface seems harsh and severe and demanding, so you may be surprised that I would offer this closing word which I believe is the core of Jesus' teaching. *Here is a mighty call to faith in the grace of God.*

Now, I believe that for two reasons. One, the context in which the story is set. The disciples have made the request in verse 5, "Lord, increase our faith!" It is then that Jesus tells the story of the grain of mustard seed, showing how important it is for us to have faith and the mighty things that result from faith.

Then, he adds this story of the harsh master and the unworthy servant. He is telling both of these stories in response to the disciples' request to increase their faith.

The second reason I believe this passage is a mighty call to faith in the grace of God is that we are driven by this word to know that nothing we can do can satisfy the righteous demands of God. This is what I suggested earlier when I said that this teaching of Jesus saves us from the sin of self-righteousness. Paul put it so sharply, "None is righteous—no, not one," and Isaiah tells us, "Our righteous deeds are like a polluted garment" (Isa. 64:6).

Note the precise words of Jesus: "When you have done all that is commanded you, say, 'We are unworthy servants; we have only done what was our duty.' " It is one thing for me to judge myself, it is another thing for Jesus to do so.

Here is the strange, yet exhilarating core of the gospel. The disciples ask, "Lord, increase our faith." Jesus responds by telling a story of a hard taskmaster and clinching that story with a soul-shaking call for us to see ourselves as unprofitable servants. He was pressing his disciples and us to make operable in our lives the great truth that as Alexander Maclaren says in *Expositions of Holy Scripture*, "in us there is nothing that can make a claim upon God, and that we must cast ourselves, as deserving nothing, wholly into his merciful hands, and find ourselves held up by his great unmerited love. Get the bitter poison root of self-trust out of you, and then there is some chance of getting the wholesome emotion of absolute reliance on Him into you."

Maclaren, whose agile mind gleaned from this text this rich, illuminating insight, used an earthy metaphor to drive home

◇ **7.**
Reflect on this assertion of Maclaren. In what way is it a blessed thing to call ourselves "unprofitable servants"?

◇ **8.**
We have not discussed one of the lessons in this word of Jesus set in the context of the parable. It has to do with external and internal compulsion. Commonly, duty is seen as an external compulsion. There is a sense in which in Jesus' message, and in the life he offers us, love replaces duty as the motivating force of our life. It is often true that the person who thinks in terms of duty tries to figure out how little he can do. The person motivated by love can never do enough. Yet, Jesus told the parable.

Reflect on the harmonizing of love and duty—how being responsible in duty can be a gracious response rather than a frantic drivenness when love is present.

◇ **9.**

For the kingdom of heaven is like a householder who went out early in the morning to hire laborers into his vineyard. After agreeing with the laborers for a denarius a day, he sent them into his vineyard. And going out about the third hour he saw others standing idle in the market place; and to them he said, "You go into the vineyard too, and whatever is right I will give you." So they went. Going out again about the sixth hour and the ninth hour, he did the same. And about the eleventh hour he went out and found others standing; and he said to them, "Why do you stand here idle all day?" They said to him, "Because no one has hired us." He said to them, "You go into the vineyard too." And when evening came, the owner of the vineyard said to his steward, "Call the laborers and pay them their wages, beginning with the last, up to the first." And when those hired about the eleventh hour came, each of them received a denarius. Now when the first came, they thought they would receive more; but each of them also received a denarius. And on receiving it they grumbled at the householder, saying, "These last worked only one hour, and you have made them equal to us who have borne the burden of the day and the scorching heat." But he replied to one of them, "Friend, I am doing you no wrong; did you not agree with me for a denarius? Take what belongs to you, and go; I choose to give to this last as I give to you. Am I not allowed to do what I choose with what belongs to me? Or do you begrudge my generosity?" So the last will be first, and the first last.

—Matthew 20:1-16

the point. He said that in these words, Jesus pricks the bladder, the float, the balloon of self-confidence which we have been using to keep our heads above water. It is only when this balloon is pricked, and we, like the apostle Peter, feel ourselves beginning to sink, that we fling out our hand to Jesus, and clutch his outstretched hand, crying, "Lord, save me!" (see Matt. 14:30).

So Jesus is responding to the disciples' request to increase their faith by saying to them that duty is perennial and our own righteousness, no matter how noble and admirable it may be, establishes no claim whatever upon God.

Our oldest daughter, Kim, the mother of our grandson, Nathan, is in theology school at Yale University. She is working part-time in youth and adult ministry in the United Methodist church of Hartford. Shortly after taking the job, the pastor invited her to preach. She simply used the lectionary lesson assigned for that Sunday. The Gospel lesson for that Sunday was one of the most difficult parables of Jesus, the one about the farmer who recruited workers and paid all of them the same amount at the end of the day, even though some of them had come at the eleventh hour. It's not an easy lesson to appropriate—that workers who work only one hour get as much pay as those who had toiled long and hard all day long.

◇ **9.**

Kim sent me a copy of her sermon, and I was pleased and surprised with the way she interpreted that passage. Her theme was that God's love and grace are offered to us without regard for our worthiness or unworthiness. That's the paradox of the gospel, seen in the sharp contrast of the vineyard owner's treatment of his workers and the attitude of those workers. The vineyard owner chose to meet the needs of the last workers just as he met the needs of the workers who toiled all day. Therefore, all the workers were able to feed their families at the end of the day. No one was mistreated. And so it is with God. Our merits or our deeds are not what forms the basis of God's love for us; it is our need and our response.

Kim used the story of her son (our grandson) Nathan's healing to illustrate the whole matter of unmerited grace. I share the story as she told it to her congregation.

Most of you have met my son, Nathan. He's a year old now, a very healthy, happy little boy. But when he was three months old, we noticed that his eyes appeared to be moving around a lot, never quite focusing on anything. So we took him to a pediatric ophthamologist who told us that Nathan had a congenital problem called nystagmus and that his eyes would basically always be that way. He then dilated Nathan's eyes and looked inside. Very matter of factly, he went on to say that Nathan had another congenital problem called optic nerve hypoplasia, a very rare defect in which his optic nerves were only about half the size they needed to be in order to see normally.

"What did that mean?" we asked. "Oh, well, of course," he

went on as though he was discussing the weather, "he'll never be able to see normally. It's an incorrectable problem, and he'll probably have to go to a special school and things like that. But don't be too worried; sometimes it's only minor and they can go to regular school and sit in front of the class and things like that."

And things like that? I thought, *What! Are you crazy? This is my son you're talking about.*

Well, we went through lots of tests and basically it was confirmed that Nathan had this problem, but people always acted very amazed at how well he seemed to be doing. Well, when we moved to Hartford, we followed up with a doctor here. I brought Nathan's records, and he examined him and was very pleased with the outcome. I felt reassured but not overly excited. And then he dilated Nathan's eyes. "Great," he said, "these optic nerves look nice and pink and healthy."

What? I thought. *Say that again!* I almost dropped Nathan in astonishment. I suggested that maybe he needed to read the first doctor's report more closely. After all, that doctor had used words like "thin" and "white" to describe the optic nerves.

Well, the doctor was amazed, because what he saw and what the first doctor reported were on opposite poles. And not only that, but the nystagmus that supposedly would never disappear had diminished remarkably. And now, while it is still there, it is not always very noticeable.

Of course, in the world of medicine, there must be confirmation as well as explanation. So we went to a third doctor to get his opinion, and he too agreed that there was no optic nerve hypoplasia. They were both baffled as to the drastic difference. But somehow, after the initial surprise wore off, I didn't feel very baffled. On the surface it appeared that the original doctor had made a mistake. Nathan hadn't been exactly helpful during the exam; in fact, he had been quite angry that he had had the audacity to try to hold him down. So maybe the doctor didn't see clearly. But that's a drastic diagnosis to make if you didn't see very clearly. And he was an awfully good doctor, highly regarded in the medical circles; the doctors here even know him. Could this be more than a mistake? Could this be the grace of God?

When Nathan was first diagnosed, we told our friends and family, who in turn told their friends and families. Soon we were receiving letters from *all over the world* saying that Nathan was being included in the daily prayers of many, many people. Could this also be an example of the power of prayer?

I realize that I'm treading on difficult ground here as I touch on the topic of the power of prayer. However, I'm reminded of our Old Testament lesson today, "For my thoughts are not your thoughts, neither are your ways my ways, says the Lord" (Isa. 55:8). There is a divine mystery here that we cannot fathom in human terms. We cannot reduce God to a human scale, nor can we assume that because events such as this do not happen all the time, they don't happen at all.

But I told this story for a reason. I believe that Nathan received God's grace. I believe my husband, John, and I received God's grace. *And it had nothing to do with merit.* I know that if merit was the deciding factor, I would not even be standing before you today, and

◇ **10.**

Nathan Söderblom said, "Only with God's good hand and strict bridle can the soul be helped to give its best." Reflect on those two images, "God's good hand" and God's "strict bridle." Write two paragraphs about how God has acted in both ways in your life to help you give your best.

Nathan's eyes would not have been healed, because my life is as stained and tarnished as anyone else's. And what great work could Nathan have done at his young age that could possibly have deserved God's grace? That is the beauty and the paradox of grace: God does not demand that we *earn* his blessings. The grace and love of God transcend our human ability to understand. But even without understanding we are called to accept that gift of grace, freely given, and rejoice. Amen.

So here it is, the core of the gospel: It is not our merit that releases God's grace. It's not even our need, because all of us stand in the same need. It is our awareness of our need, the acknowledgment that we are "unworthy servants," deserving nothing. We place ourselves wholly into the merciful hands of God, and we find ourselves saved and held up by God's great unmerited love.   ◇ **10**

CHAPTER ◇ 7

A New Look at the Sabbath

By law, the Tokyo City Zoo in Japan must be closed for two days each month. The law was necessary because officials discovered that the animals were showing signs of extreme emotional distress from being constantly exposed to the public.

If that is true of animals, how much more is it true of us humans? We are constantly under stress, especially as we are exposed to the public. We need to take time—time to rest our bodies, time to let our minds slow down, time to give some ease to our souls, time to reflect and pray, time to worship, time to join ourselves in quality relationships with those who love us.

One of the Ten Commandments lays down the law "Remember the sabbath day, to keep it holy" (Exod. 20:8). The concept of sabbath must be critically important, judging by the attention it gets and the controversy it sparks, not only in the Old Testament, but in the New Testament as well. Further, it is clear that observance of the sabbath encompasses the entire community of God—it applies not only to God's people, but to their servants and their beasts of burden as well. As you can see, the practice of the Tokyo City Zoo is well-grounded in scripture! Just what is it about the sabbath that makes it so vital? That is what we will be doing in this chapter—taking a new look at the sabbath.

Some of you may grin at the title of this chapter, "A New Look at the Sabbath." *Any* look is a new look. I started to title it "Another Look," but many of us have not taken a serious first look.

The congregation I serve in Memphis, Tennessee, is blessed by a wide variety of age groups and religious backgrounds. There are many people with very disciplined religious experiences and many at the other end of the spectrum, hardly any religious experience or tradition at all. We're blessed with a large number of young adults and young married couples in our congregation.

I could not recall a pattern of sabbath practice with which all in the congregation could identify. ◇ **1.** In rural Mississippi, where I grew up, everybody knew what Sunday was for. It

◇ **1.**
Reflect on your early life. Make some notes about how you celebrated Sunday in your family when you were a child.

53

◇ **2.**

Reflect for a moment on the changes that have come in your life and in the way the sabbath is celebrated now compared to the way you recall it as a child.

◇ **3.**

One sabbath he was going through the grainfields; and as they made their way his disciples began to pluck heads of grain. And the Pharisees said to him, "Look, why are they doing what is not lawful on the sabbath?" And he said to them, "Have you never read what David did, when he was in need and was hungry, he and those who were with him: how he entered the house of God, when Abiathar was high priest, and ate the bread of the Presence which it is not lawful for any but the priests to eat, and also gave it to those who were with him?" And he said to them, "The sabbath was made for man, not man for the sabbath; so the Son of man is lord even of the sabbath."

—Mark 2:23-28

was for going to church. That is, it was for going to church if it was the first or the third Sunday, because those were the only Sundays we had a preacher. He was somewhere else the other two Sundays. Sunday was also for visiting relatives. It was for children to gather in the afternoon for games.

What it wasn't for was any kind of work. Nor was it for playing cards or going to the movies. I remember the first movie I went to on Sunday afternoon—without the knowledge of my parents. My conscience hurt me for months.

There were certain recreational things that, even though you did them on other days, you didn't do on Sunday. Playing cards is a good example of that. We never played cards on Sunday. Our favorite family game back then was Rook. And I remember going home for vacation long after I had become a preacher and married. On Sunday afternoon, our family was playing cards (my mother and father had become a bit more liberal at that point) when the Baptist preacher, their pastor, drove up. I will never forget my mother's frantic effort to get us to stop the card game and put the cards up before the preacher "caught us." So, it was clear what we did and did not do on Sunday.

How many of you remember the long fights that occurred twenty five and thirty years ago about blue laws, laws that prohibited the opening of businesses and entertainment establishments on Sunday. I remember some of those fights when I was a student preacher, even before I entered seminary. Naturally, I was opposed to the Sunday opening of stores, but I remember one particular Sunday morning which was a Communion Sunday. I awakened to the fact that I had failed to get grape juice the previous day, and I was responsible for bringing the grape juice and preparing for the Communion service. With a lowered head and deep chagrin, I went to a small curb market that had opened on Sunday and bought some juice so that we could have Communion. In those blue-law debates and battles, we were trying to preserve a culture that would at least "nod approval" to the commandment "Remember the sabbath day and keep it holy."   ◇ **2.**

Traditionally, we think of the misuse of the sabbath by the extreme secularization of it, turning it into just another day. For a vast portion of our population, there is no hint of the sacred in it. But Jesus addressed the misuse of the sabbath from another perspective. If we have made it too secular, the Pharisees had made it too sacred. So Jesus said, "The sabbath was made for man, not man for the sabbath." Yes, *That's What The Man Said.* So I want us to look at both problems and support a larger notion of sabbath time without which we cannot know wholeness.   ◇ **3.**

First, mark this down as our starting point. The sabbath is a gift of God.

Now, as we know, the Christian's Sunday is different from the sabbath that is talked about in scripture. The Christian Sunday is a gift of the church. It may shock you to learn that Jesus gives no specific command regarding the observance of what is now the Christian sabbath. In his book on worship, *With Glad and Generous Hearts,* William H. Willimon gives us something of the history.

> The first Jewish Christians continued to "remember the sabbath day, to keep it holy" by attending the synagogue as Jesus had done before them (Luke 4:16). Then, on Sunday, the first day of the Jewish work week, they gathered with their Christian brothers and sisters at church, probably in the evening as soon as they gof off work. Eventually, relations between the Jews in the synagogue and those who were now Christians became strained. Jewish Christians were evicted from the synagogues, and Christianity, which had originally been a sectarian movement within Judaism, became a distinct religion (Willimon, pp. 16-17).

What had begun among the early Christians as a remembrance of the Resurrection, by the third century had become a legal holiday, the Christian sabbath. What is important is not whether we observe the sabbath on the first or the seventh day, but that we observe it without fail.

Although the Christian Sunday as the day of worship is a gift of the church, the change that has come in sabbath observance—or the lack of sabbath observance—has not been under the leadership of the church. Commenting on this dilemma, Clovis Chappell observes that, caught in the strong currents of the world, churched and unchurched alike have lost this once holy day. He suggests that we have not thought our way to this change, but rather, we have "drifted into it under the spell of the worship of the twin gods of pleasure and gold." ◇ **4.**

Now let's look at the specific problem Jesus is addressing. The problem goes beyond how we observe Sunday. Here is the ongoing pervasive problem of turning means into ends. It's really a problem of idolatry. This New Testament story will paint the picture clearly.

> Now there is in Jerusalem by the Sheep Gate a pool, in Hebrew called Bethzatha, which has five porticoes. In these lay a multitude of invalids, blind, lame, paralyzed. One man was there, who had been ill for thirty-eight years. When Jesus saw him and knew that he had been lying there a long time, he said to him, "Do you want to be healed?" The sick man answered him, "Sir, I have no man to put me into the pool when the water is troubled, and while I am going another steps down before me." Jesus said to him, "Rise, take up your pallet and walk." And at once the man was healed, and he took up his pallet and walked. Now that day was the sabbath. So the Jews said to the man who was cured, "It is the sabbath, it is not lawful for you to carry your pallet." But he

◇ **4.**
Reflect on these questions:
Do you see Sunday as a holy day?

Apart from corporate worship, what sets your Sunday apart from other days?

Do you have any guilt about the use you make of Sunday?

If you had the power to influence the whole of society, how would you design the celebration of Sunday?

How has pleasure and materialism shaped how you celebrate Sunday?

answered them, "The man who healed me said to me, "Take up your pallet, and walk." They asked him, "Who is the man who said to you, "Take up your pallet, and walk?"

—John 5:2-12

It's hard for us to imagine this, but it's there in scripture. It would seem more logical to want to know, "How were you healed?" or "Who healed you?" But, those who were there were blinded by their rigid legalism. They missed the miracle altogether. They only asked, "Who told you to carry your pallet?" They were not interested in the healing of this man. They were only interested in keeping of the sabbath. By putting institutional values above human values, they had a distorted, even perverted understanding, and so they misused the sabbath. They turned means into ends. This wrong sense of values continues to work tragedy in our day.

Erma Bombeck is one of my favorite writers. Some time ago she shared a vignette that has provided me many a chuckle as I have recalled it since first reading it. She said that she was in church one Sunday morning when a little child on the row in front of her began turning around and smiling at everyone in the pews behind him. He wasn't gurgling or spitting or humming or kicking, neither was he tearing the hymnal pages or rummaging through his mother's purse. He was just smiling happily and spreading his warmth to all those around him.

All of a sudden, wrote Erma, his mother realized what he was doing and jerked him around angrily. In a stage whisper that could be heard several pews away, she said, "Stop that grinning— you're in church!" And then she whacked him soundly on the bottom. When she did, of course, great big tears began to roll down his cheeks, and the little boy started to cry. And do you know what the mother said? "That's better. Now let's start worshipping God again."

You get the picture. Where did we ever get the idea that laughter and joy have no place in the church? Who has promoted the notion that when we relate to God we must be somber and stern and very stiff? Can anyone tell me where we get the idea that being holy means being somber? Being Christian doesn't even mean "being religious." If anything lies at the heart of our faith, it is joy!

We're always distorting values and misusing that which has been given to us to enrich our lives. This is true not only of our use of Sunday but our use of other institutions as well. I think we must all agree with Clovis Chappell when he says that "no institution, either secular or religious, has a right to exist save as it builds up and conserves human values."

"The sabbath was made for man, not man for the sabbath." *That's What the Man Said!* ◇ **5.**

It was no wonder that Jesus spoke his word. The Pharisees had reached the conclusion that humanity was made for the sab-

◇ **5.**
Take a few moments for reflection, then list those instances in which we sometimes place institutional values above human values in our families, in our workplace, in our community, in our government, in our church, in the world at large? How might a deeper understanding of sabbath affect those areas? Make some notes here.

bath, not the sabbath for humanity. They hedged the day about with many restrictions. It became a day of repression rather than a day of expression, or, as Chappel says, "a day of don'ts rather than a day of do's. There were so many petty things that were forbidden on the sabbath that it took a learned man to know them all. For instance, if one were bitten by a flea in the sabbath he was not allowed to catch and exterminate a pest lest he should be guilty of desecrating the holy day by hunting. Thus they changed the day, for many, from a blessing into a burden."   ◇ **6.**

"The sabbath was made for man, not man for the sabbath." *That's What the Man Said,* because he believed in the sabbath as a means to an end, not as an end in itself. To him, the supreme values were always human values. He determined the worth of every institution by one test: its power to serve and enrich the whole life of persons.

Let me draw two very practical applications from what Jesus said. The first concerns our celebrating the Christian sabbath by attending worship. We attend church not in the spirit of people performing a religious duty but in the spirit of people who feel that their attendance at worship is a loud, living *Amen* to the conviction that the sabbath is made for people.

Our tithes and offerings contribute to the support of hospitals and of homes for the orphans and aged. They help feed those threatened by starvation and assist refugees. They support a host of other charitable endeavors as a concrete expression of our conviction that the right observance is to help and to save life.

We feel that our participation in the sabbath worship will help us and save our life. It will help us to become convicted of our sins. It will inspire us to do for others as we would have them do for us. It will undergird us with the conviction that we can be rooted and grounded in God's love and the sure knowledge that God is for us.

It is here in worship that our hearts can be cleansed, a right spirit renewed within us, and the intention kindled to lead a new life. It is here that we hear the unforgettable call of Christ, "Take up your cross and follow me." There's something about this Jesus, who believes that the sabbath is made for man, and that we celebrate it correctly when we help and save life, that captures our imagination, quickens our hearts, and excites our mind. (H. Brack, p. 53)

There is a further implication that I want to draw from Jesus' words about the sabbath that has to do with how we do our work and how we live out our vocations from day to day. This dimension is important to us because what Jesus is saying about the sabbath he is saying about life: all that we do should have about it a commitment to sharing the love of Christ and bringing wholeness to others.

I was listening to a taped meditation on Matthew 12:1-12 by Dr. Stephen Brown. He quoted a poem written by an elderly lady

◇ **6.**
David McKenna has said, "Most families would have to confess that the Pharisees have lost but Jesus has not won the struggle to interpret the Biblical principle of the Sabbath which God intended."

Is that true? Reflect on what Dr. McKenna is saying.

who died in a hospital near Dundee, England. Her poem is about how nurses and others who care for the elderly should see them. The poem was found after the woman's death.

> What do you see, nurses, what do you see?
> Are you thinking of me when you look at me?
> A crabbish old lady not very wise,
> uncertain of habit with faraway eyes.
> Who dribbles her food and makes no reply
> when you say in a loud voice, "I do wish you'd try."

> Who seems not to notice the things that you drop,
> and forever is losing a stocking or sock,
> who unresisting or not lets you do as you will
> with bathing and feeding the long day to fill. Is that
> what you're thinking? Is that what you see?
> Then open your eyes, Nurse, you're not looking at me.

The woman then recited the story of her full and busy life, recalling youth and marriage, children and grandchildren. She concludes:

> I'm an old woman now; nature is cruel;
> 'Tis her just to make old age look like a fool.
> The body, it crumbles; grace and vigor depart,
> There's a stone where once I had a heart.
> But inside this old carcass a young girl still dwells;
> and now and again, my battered heart swells.
> I remember the joys, I remember the pain;
> And I'm loving and living life over again.
> So open your eyes, nurses, open and see.
> Not a crabbish old woman, look closer—
> Look at me.

Isn't that poignant? And the lesson to the nurses in a nursing home is a lesson to all of us—all that we do should have about it the commitment to sharing the love of Christ and bringing wholeness to others. *That's What the Man Said*. "The sabbath was made for man, not man for the sabbath."

Roger Bannister, an Englishman who ran the mile in less than four minutes, tells of standing on the beach and being struck by the awesome beauty and perfection of nature. The emotion that arose in him found its expression in running. When standing he felt like an observer, but when he was running he felt united with the natural beauty around him.

Commenting on that story, Harold A. Brack said,

> Our observance of the Sabbath is like that. If we only come weekly to properly participate in the ritual acts, we feel like an observer. But when we enter into the work of [salvation], then we feel united with that gracious love of God that gave an only son to suffer death upon the cross for our redemption and, while we were yet sinners, died for us.

In our work of helping and saving we become a living expression of the great good news, "The Sabbath is made for man!" (Brack, p. 54) ◇ **7.**

We need a day set apart for worship, for rest, for the family; we need a break in the pace of the week.

For multitudes of us today, both within the church and without, the Sabbath is largely a lost gift. We've lost it by simply leaving it alone, for in order to lose our Sabbath, we don't have to preach against it; we don't have to repeal all laws regarding it; all we have to do is to treat it as we treat any other day. "The Sabbath was made for man." If this is true, then to claim that this Sabbath is to be used just as we use every other day is to accuse Jesus of talking nonsense. If we do not use the Sabbath in a different fashion from that in which we use other days, then we're refusing to accept God's good gift.

Of course I'm aware of the arguments against this. We say that everyday ought to be holy unto the Lord, and that is true, but the man who observes the Sabbath is far more likely to observe the other days as holy than the man who does not. The same argument is used against going to church. "Everyplace," we claim, "ought to be a holy place." Yet the man who has no special place for worship is very likely not to find a holy place anywhere. To treat the Sabbath, therefore, as we treat every other day is to lose it, and in losing it to help rob ourselves and our fellows as well. (Chappell, p. 90)

Did you hear the story of the preacher who really was addicted to golf? He played golf three or four times every week. One week he had been able to play golf only twice. Sunday came, and he pretended to be sick, called for a substitute at church, and slipped away to play golf by himself.

He was blithely playing along, and he hit a long shot. Miraculously, it was a hole in one. St. Peter and God were looking down at this preacher, who was playing hookey and lying to his congregation. St. Peter couldn't stand it. "Are you going to let him get away with that? Why didn't you prevent him from making that hole in one?"

"Prevent him?" God said. "I made it for him!"

"Why? Why in the world would you let him play such a magnificent game and make a hole-in-one? Instead, you should be punishing him!"

God said, "That is his punishment. Think about never being able to tell anybody about making a hole-in-one, when you make it, and how?"

We need our Sundays. And we need to keep our Sundays for worship, rest, and family—a break in the pace. But I want to make a larger plea—a plea for sabbath time.

We need a rhythm in our life that includes involvement and disengagement; action and retreat. We need time where we simply

◇ **7.**
Moral development is a concern of contemporary psychology and education. Lawrence Kohlberg of Harvard University is one of the leaders in the field. On a six-stage scale of moral development, he makes this the lowest level: a person does what is right because of the fear of punishment.

In the last chapter we talked about duty. Sabbath-keeping is one of the laws of the Ten Commandments, it is a duty. To what degree do you think the Pharisees' rigid requirement of law and punishment and the way the church has interpreted the sabbath and other duties since have contributed to the loss of positive understanding of law and duty?

Reflect on this for a few minutes.

According to Kohlberg's six-stage scale of moral development, at the highest level, *a person chooses* what is right—not because of fear or reward, but because of belief in a moral principle. How can we translate this into a challenging message from the church as it relates to what we might commonly call "religious duties?" Write three or four sentences.

◇ **8.**

How would you have to change your lifestyle to incorporate times for "doing nothing for God's sake and ours"?

do nothing, for God's sake and ours. Consider these words from the hymn "Dear Lord and Father of Mankind" as a model and a prayer:

> O sabbath by Galilee!
> O calm of hills above,
> Where Jesus knelt to share with thee
> The silence of eternity,
> Interpreted by love!
>
> Drop thy still dews of quietness,
> Till all our strivings cease;
> Take from our souls the strain and stress,
> And let our ordered lives confess
> The beauty of Thy peace.

◇ **8.**

In his book *Sabbath Time,* Tilden Edwards, with painful clarity, puts his finger on our common condition:

> The task, imposed on us by both our culture and ourselves, has an edge of anxiety and striving violence to it. We believe that it is up to us to get and to keep who we are . . .
> [There is a shift] to defining ourselves (and being defined by others) in terms of what we *produce* through whatever individual way of life this production of self and things may involve. Today we could also include what we *consume* as part of our identity: our consumption of education, material goods, public events, passive hobbies, etc. Such consumptive activity can involve as much drivenness as our productivity.
> This individualized way of life, even during leisure time, produces enormous pressure on us. When it becomes too much we are tempted to collapse into some form of oblivion: sleep, drink, drugs, any kind of television, or whatever else might numb our self-production for a while.
> The rhythm of life for countless people, set by this culturally pressured way, thus emerges as one that oscillates between driven achievement (both on and off the job) and some form of mind-numbing private escape. This crazed rhythm, based on a distorted view of human reality, increasingly poisons our institutions, relationships, and quality of life (Edwards, p. 4).

Like the animals of the Tokyo City Zoo, we, too, show signs of extreme emotional distress from being constantly exposed to the public. And, we are too little exposed to the healing presence of God. We need the sabbath time that we carry within us, an attitude that hallows all of life, a gentle turning of the heart toward God. From our condition of drivenness, we must learn to take for ourselves sabbath time, that time in which we do nothing for God's sake and ours. Without such time, it is little wonder that we do not hear God speaking to us. It is little wonder that our spirits become dry and our values distorted. It is little wonder that we do not experience wholeness within ourselves and have difficulty in helping others find wholeness.

Although we are familiar with the sabbath commandment from Exodus which emphasizes God's rhythm of labor and rest in the creation, there is another reference to this commandment in Deuteronomy. The Deuteronomy account has a slightly different emphasis—here the celebration of the sabbath has the added dimension of reminding the Hebrews of their deliverance from bondage by the hand of God. The work of salvation and redemption was God's work; the Hebrews had only to be themselves—God's people. Following the Exodus they were reminded by the sabbath that by the power of God they had been set free from that which enslaved them. In a very real sense, our sabbath time can be the means by which we, through the power of God, are no longer held captive by our busyness, the encumbrances of daily life, outside pressures and chaos. Loretta Girzaitis invites us into sabbath time:

> Sometimes, we take the initiative in prayer: pleading, praising, thanking, worshipping. At other times, God demands our attention by disturbing our indifference, penetrating our hardened hearts, and claiming our space and time.
>
> Then there is a sabbath of prayer—a period of rest and quiet when our beings relax totally in God's presence. We enjoy the company of the Lord with delight and satisfaction.
>
> During this sabbath time, the soul works not at all. But the Eternal is very active—challenging, cleansing, purifying, loving. This activity lures the beloved into the embrace of the great lover, where both rest together as one.
>
> The mind, the heart, and the spirit are energized with grace. We need but absorb this courtesy like a sponge, permitting God's activity to fill the empty spaces of our beings (Girzaitis, p. 48). ◇ **9.**

◇ **9.**
Reflect on the possibilities of "a sabbath of prayer." Is prayer a "sabbath time" for you?

CHAPTER ◇ 8

Not Servants But Friends

◇ **1.**

As the Father has loved me, so have I loved you; abide in my love. If you keep my commandments, you will abide in my love, just as I have kept my Father's commandments and abide in his love. These things I have spoken to you, that my joy may be in you, and that your joy may be full.

This is my commandment, that you love one another as I have loved you. Greater love has no man than this, that a man lay down his life for his friends. You are my friends if you do what I command you. No longer do I call you servants, for the servant does not know what his master is doing; but I have called you friends, for all that I have heard from my Father I have made known to you. You did not choose me, but I chose you and appointed you that you should go and bear fruit and that your fruit should abide; so that whatever you ask the Father in my name, he may give it to you. This I command you, to love one another.

—John 15:9-17

A man was hiking in the mountains. He ventured out on a precipice to immerse himself in the unutterable beauty of a panoramic picture of nature. The ground gave way beneath him, and he found himself plunging down a cliff. Part of the way down he grabbed a branch which strained to support him. He didn't know how long the branch would hold. There he was hanging in the air with a rushing stream and big rocks at least a thousand feet below. You can imagine his desperation. He sucked in just enough breath to lift a prayer toward what he thought was the general direction of heaven.

"Is anybody up there?" There was no answer. "*Please*," he pleaded, "Is anybody up there? If so, please speak to me."

Just as he felt the final ounces of strength ebbing from his body, a voice responded, "Yes, I am here."

"Good, thank God! Please save me."

The voice came back, "I will. I will save you, but you will have to trust me. First of all, you must let go of the branch."

There was a long, long silence as the man continued to hold desperately to the branch and looked down at the rushing waters and the rocks a thousand feet below. Finally, he cried out again, "Is anybody *else* up there?"

That's the way it is, isn't it? One of our biggest questions is that one. Maybe it is not voiced in precisely the same way and certainly it does not always come from such desperate situations; but our question is, "Is anybody up there?"

And there is a second question that we ask. *"Who* is the Anybody up there? What is the 'Anybody up there' like?" ◇ **1.**

Henry Jordan was a great all-pro tackle who played with the Green Bay Packers back in the heyday of Coach Vince Lombardi. He was as good with words as he was at sacking quarterbacks. This made him a favorite with sportswriters. One of his widely quoted statements came when somebody tried to determine if his coach was prejudiced.

"Did Mr. Lombardi show any preference to blacks or

62

whites?" he was asked. "No, sir," Jordan answered. "He treats all of us the same—like dogs."

What is the nature of God—does God treat us all the same? How does God see us? And what does God treat us like?

The section of scripture we are considering in this chapter, John 15:9-17, addresses all these questions—Someone *is* up there; that Someone loves us, and in fact, that Someone calls us friends.

I think, for me, there is no more beautiful word spoken by Jesus, no word that gratifies my soul more than this one: "No longer do I call you servants . . . I have called you friends." *That's What the Man Said.*

The setting of this word is important. What Jesus has already said sets the stage for this soothing assurance which he gives to his followers. In John 15:1-8 he has used the beautiful metaphor of the vine and the branches in which he tells us who he is in relation to God and who we are in relation to him. And Jesus repeats it more than once, "I am the vine, you are the branches. He who abides in me, and I in him, he it is that bears much fruit, for apart from me you can do nothing."

Jesus went on to talk about what this meant, this vine-branch relationship, with the Father as the vine-dresser. "As the Father has loved me, so have I loved you; abide in my love" (v. 9). He then reiterated that in verse 12: "This is my commandment, that you love one another as I have loved you." And then Jesus really underscored what that meant in verse 13: "Greater love has no man than this, that a man lay down his life for his friends."

The reason we can listen to what Jesus said is because he confirmed his words with his life. We know what happened. He laid down his life for his friends—for you and me. We can believe Jesus' word because his actions confirmed them.

Before we move to our particular focus on friendship, let's register an important point: When the Christian faith tries to define love, it points squarely to Jesus Christ hanging on a cross.

The Cross is God's word to us: This is how much I love you.

There's nothing in it for God. What do you think God got out of it? Only the confirmation of God's nature, which is love. God simply loved the world so much that he gave his Son.

I doubt if any word in our language is more abused than *love*. It can mean everything, or it can mean nothing. It may be impossible for us to accept the audacity of the gospel, which simply says that *God is love*. Our starting point has to be a reversal of our normal way of thinking. Instead of love defining God, we begin with a more fundamental fact: God defines love.

Thus, our beginning point. When the Christian faith tries to define love, it points to Jesus Christ hanging on a cross. This is God's definition.

That's a powerful image—the image of the love which God defines in sacrificing himself in Jesus Christ to die on a cross.

But as that kind of love that God defines has a divine face, it also has a human face as well. That love is demonstrated over and over again in people you and I know. One of the great United Methodist preachers of America is a man named David Seamands. For many years he was the pastor of the United Methodist church in Wilmore, Kentucky, and before that he was a missionary in India. He now teaches pastoral care at Asbury Theological Seminary.

When he and his wife, Helen, were missionaries in India, their son, Steve, was born. Steve is now a professor of theology, a perfect physical specimen, and still an outstanding soccer player. But when he was born, one foot was severely clubfooted. Because of the distance between the village where his parents were serving in India and the closest orthopedic specialist, the club foot got a head start on them. It took twelve years, three major surgeries, and two and one-half years in a cast to straighten out the foot. There came the time, as it comes with every child, when they could no longer keep him in a cast. One day the doctor called his parents in and said to them, "You are going to have to take over the therapy." Let me tell the story from that point in David's words:

> Following the doctor's careful instructions, every day Helen and I had to hold Steve down on a padded table and, placing his foot over a bottle, by sheer force I had to turn it back in the opposite direction. I had to over-correct it, over-straighten it in the right direction as far as it had been turned in the wrong direction. Steve was a tiny boy at the time and had absolutely no way of understanding what we were doing. You can imagine his response. He begged us to stop. And when we didn't stop, he would scream out in pain. I think the hardest part was when in his pain and anger, he would shout his hatred of me. My stomach would churn, and I would literally go away sick from the whole business. I think the only thing that kept us going was the doctor's word to us, "If you don't want your son to be a cripple, make sure you keep it up every day."

David concluded the story by saying, "I don't need to explain to any parent what it cost us to do it. But when he got to be a teenager and when I used to watch him win all of those high school and college (soccer) tournaments, and when I see him walking now without the slightest limp, I say to myself, 'It was awfully hard, but it was worth it all.'"   ◇ **2.**

So that's where we begin—with the love that God defines, that love acted out by Jesus on the cross, confirming his claim, "Greater love has no man than this, that a man lay down his life for his friends."

Jesus lingers on that idea. He knew that it is too great and too sweet a truth to be taken in all at once. So, with a remarkable reiteration to drive the point home, he speaks that most wonderful word in verse 15: "No longer do I call you servants, for the servant

◇ **2.**
Name here the three persons you know who reflect love most clearly.

_____

_____

_____

What about the love of these persons makes it the *love which God defines*. Put down words or phrases that describe that love.

does not know what his master is doing; but I have called you friends, for all that I have heard from my Father I have made known to you." *That's What the Man Said!*

What a word! What a fact! Can we comprehend it? Will we accept it? What might it mean to us if we did?

Since there is so much more here than we can ever appropriate, let's simply stick with the basics, get that clear in our minds, then spend the rest of our lives working on it.

The beginning then is to ask, How does it all come about? How do we become friends of Christ? In case you missed it, it's there in verse 16: "You did not choose me, but I chose you."

What a foundation stone for friendship—"being chosen!" Chosen by Christ to be his friend. That's the first answer to how we become friends of Christ—he has chosen us.

There's really nothing like knowing that we are chosen.

◇ **3.**

A busy business executive turned to a young man carrying a briefcase and said to him, "Son, you ought to feel mighty flattered. I've refused to see twelve other salesmen who have wanted to talk to me today."

"I know," replied the young salesman, "I'm all twelve of them!"

He was chosen by his own persistence.

Then there was the young man who was a top salesman for a dress company. The owner of the company, very impressed by this young man asked him if he would like to be a partner in the clothing business. The fellow enthusiastically replied that he would. The owner then said, "You'll have to marry one of my daughters. You know the two who are sitting in the other room. You've seen them a lot. You've not met Rebecca, but she'll be here shortly." The young man thought for only a moment of the two girls he knew and then said, "I'll take Rebecca."

There's nothing like it—being chosen. Do you get the impact of this? Has it really dawned on you in the fullness of its power? Christ has chosen you.

So, that's the first part of our answer to the question how do we become friends of Christ? We have been chosen.　◇ **4.**

We find a second aspect of our friendship with Christ in our scripture lesson. Look at verse 14: "You are my friends if you do what I command you."

In verse 13 Jesus has said, "Greater love has no man than this, that a man lay down his life for his friends." *Friends* in this verse refers to those whom Jesus loved. Now in verse 13, he is talking about those who love him. They love him because he loves them. This is really two sides of the same thought, and they cannot be separated. But don't miss the big idea here. Verse 14 is presenting the idea of friendship with Christ from the human side. Jesus

◇ **3.**
Look back in your memory and recall one experience of being chosen. Write enough about that experience to get in touch with the meaning of it. What did it feel like to be chosen?

◇ **4.**
Do you feel that you have been chosen by Christ? Try to remember when you first were aware of being chosen by him. Describe in three or four sentences how you feel about being chosen.

Are you acting as though you are chosen? Do other people know that you know you are chosen?

tells us that we are his lovers, that is, that we are his friends, his disciples, as well as beloved by him, *on condition of doing his will, doing whatever he commands us*.

Does it sound tough, this word of Jesus? "You are my friends, if you do what I command you."

Here we are introduced to a very important theological issue. There are those who contend that we have no choice in our salvation, in our being chosen. The term for that is *predestination*. Perhaps, too simply put, the idea is that some of us are chosen, predestined, for salvation, while some are not; likewise, some are predestined for damnation. I agree with a part of this contention— *we have no choice in being chosen*. That's what Jesus said. "You have not chosen me, but I have chosen you." But here is the point, the crucial point: we are *all* chosen. We have no choice in that. We are all chosen—not just a few favored ones, not one or two picked out of the crowd. *In Jesus Christ, God has chosen all humankind for salvation:* "For God so loved the world [that's everybody] that he gave his only Son, that *whoever* [that's anybody who will] believes in him should not perish but have eternal life" (John 3:16). The gospel is, in the words of that old hymn, "Whosoever will may come."

But there's another crucial theological nuance here. Salvation is free, universally offered, the expression of God's grace. If we accept that gift of grace by faith, then we accept our chosenness. But that isn't all. We stay in our state of being chosen, we retain our salvation, we continue as friends of Christ as long as the turn of our soul, the bent of our life, the deep desire of our heart is to obey him. *That's What the Man Said:* "You are my friends if you do what I command you."

How can we insist on eternal security, or in the vernacular, "once saved always saved," with words like this pervading the New Testament? "You are my friends if you do what I command you."

Does that answer the question enough for you to go on? How do we become friends of Christ? We are chosen, chosen by him. But we have to accept that chosenness by faith, and we remain his friends by doing what he tells us to do.   ◇ **5.**

◇ **5.**
What are your thoughts about predestination? About "once saved always saved?"
Reflecting on recent conversations with your friends, what do they think about predestination? Eternal security?

Now a second foundational concern: *the privilege of friendship*. Notice how Jesus put it in verse 15: "No longer do I call you servants, for the servant does not know what his master is doing, but I have called you friends, for all that I have heard from my Father, I have made known to you."

Paramount in the privilege of friendship with Christ are the two greatest needs of our life: *acceptance* and *intimacy*. Our great need as social beings is to be connected. Acceptance and intimacy provide that.

Too many persons falsely think position and status will give us the meaning and connectedness we need. Sometime ago a yacht was caught in a severe winter storm in the Pacific Ocean and began to sink. The financier who owned the yacht became desperate and quickly got on the radio to call for help. He sent out one SOS after another, hoping that someone would pick up his signal. Finally, a coast-guard cutter heard him. "We are on the way," the coast guard radioed, "what is your position? We repeat, what is your position?"

Immediately the response came back, "I'm chairman of the board of First National Bank and Trust Company! Please hurry!"

There are a lot of people who are really hung up on their position in life, but position and status don't give us the acceptance and intimacy we need. All of us desperately need to feel connected. Just as position and status do not give us the connectedness we need, neither does *recognition*.

Here is a tragic story that speaks to the issue. Some of you remember the name Kathy Ormsby, the record-setting distance runner from North Carolina State University, whose life was one triumph after another. Today Kathy is paralyzed and is not expected to walk again because one evening she inexplicably jumped from a bridge during the NCAA championships in Indianapolis. Kathy Ormsby never received a grade lower than an A in twelve years of school. She graduated first in a high school class of 600 with an unprecedented 99 average. She set three state records in track, and she never gloated in victory or sulked in defeat.

Before she graduated, the mayors of five communities in her home county did something they had never done before. They declared a day in honor of a high school senior, and her fellow students and townspeople wore buttons listing Kathy's accomplishments. So why in the name of all that's reasonable did Kathy Ormsby jump from that bridge in Indianapolis? I do not know Kathy Ormsby personally and so I certainly cannot answer the question. But the tragic story underscores for me that recognition is not enough. We need *connection* and connection comes through acceptance and intimacy. ◇ **6.**

The friendship Christ offers provides acceptance and intimacy at a level no human friend can afford.

In his commentary on this word, Alexander Maclaren suggested a shocking truth: "Everyone of Christ's friends stands nearer to God than did Moses at the door of the tabernacle, when the wondering camp beheld him face to face with the blaze of the Shekinah Glory . . . . "

Have you ever thought of that? You and I can be closer to God than Moses because God has given himself to us in Jesus Christ. And Jesus says, "I take you into my life. I share my mind and heart with you. I make known to you everything I have heard from the Father." Wow!

In my preparation for this chapter, I experienced a marvelous mental and spiritual serendipity. I was not looking for this at all, and how it came to my attention I am not sure. William Ritter, a Methodist preacher in Detroit, was talking about the story of Jesus

◇ **6.**
Who are your two best friends? Write their names here.

_____

_____

Write three or four sentences about each, describing how they provide you acceptance and intimacy.

◇ **7.**
Locate in your memory your most recent experience of Jesus coming to you.
Record that experience here.

walking on the water, going to the disciples who were in their boat in the dead of night with the storm raging. He talked about how we get preoccupied with the miracle of Jesus walking on the water. Then he said:

> That whole debate misses the point of the story. I think the miracle has less to do with a Jesus who comes by impossible means than with the Jesus who comes at impossible times. When it is darkest, He comes. When we are weariest, He comes! When the sea is so wide and our boat is so small . . . when we are a day late and a dollar short— or a month late and a rent payment short . . . when the storms of life are raging . . . when we're up a creek with no paddle, and our arms are too tired to hold a paddle if we had one . . . when it's too dark to see by . . . or, worse yet, when it's too dark to hope by, Jesus comes 'round." (Ritter, September 11, 1988)

That's the privilege of friendship: acceptance and intimacy; Jesus being there for us all the time.   ◇ **7.**

Let's move to the final foundational concern: *Friends of a Friend should themselves be friends*. It's at the heart of all Jesus is teaching us. Verse 12 is underscored in different ways throughout John's Gospel and throughout the New Testament: "This is my commandment, that you love one another." Friends of a friend should themselves be friends. If we are to be friends of Jesus, we must be friends of others. We must give ourselves in love.

◇ **8.**
Go back to your notes where you wrote about your two best friends providing acceptance and love.
How did the love of your friends communicate the love of Christ?

I think of Thomas Merton, one of the great communicators of the Christian faith in our day, a man who became a Trappist monk. He didn't grow up in the faith. He had a tumultuous childhood, a turbulent youth. His life was in confusion and disarray when he went as a student to Columbia University in New York City. That setting might be the last in which you would expect a person to experience faith or conversion, but Merton says that's precisely what happened. In his autobiography, he wrote:

> Strangely enough, it was on this big factory of a campus that the Holy Ghost was waiting to show me the light, in His own light. And one of the chief means He used, and through which he operated was human friendship . . . . God brought me and a half dozen others together at Columbia, and made us friends, in such a way that our friendship would work powerfully to rescue us from the confusion and the misery in which we had come to find ourselves." (Merton, p. 177)

I said earlier that the friendship Christ offers provides acceptance and intimacy at a level no human friend can afford. Paradoxically, this friendship, Jesus' friendship, is communicated by you and me. For that reason, friends of *the* friend should themselves be friends.   ◇ **8.**

There's a wonderful story about a young girl who was walking through a meadow and saw a butterfly impaled upon a thorn. Very carefully she released it, and the butterfly started to fly away. Then it came back and changed into a beautiful good fairy. "For your kindness," she told the little girl, "I will grant you your fondest wish." The little girl thought for a moment and replied, "I want to be happy." The fairy leaned forward toward her and whispered in her ear and then suddenly vanished.

As the little girl grew, no one in the land was happier than she. When everyone asked her for the secret of her happiness, she would only smile and say, "I listened to a good fairy."

As she grew older, the neighbors were afraid the fabulous secret might die with her. "Tell us, please," they begged, "tell us what the fairy said."

The now-lovely old woman simply smiled and said, "She told me that everyone, no matter how secure they seemed, had need of me."

Acting upon the word of the good fairy, she had found happiness. So it is. As friends of our Friend Jesus, we should be friends to others. Nothing gives more powerful witness to our friendship of Christ, and nothing is more effective in bringing others to claiming their chosenness by Christ than our love. ◇ **9.**

◇ **9.**
Write the names of three persons you know who need to be loved in a special way.

_____

_____

_____

How can you love these persons so that they may claim their chosenness by Christ?

CHAPTER 9

How Deep Is Down?

◇ **1.**

Jesus knew that they wanted to ask him; so he said to them, "Is this what you are asking yourselves, what I meant by saying, 'A little while, and you will not see me, and again a little while, and you will see me'? Truly, truly, I say to you, you will weep and lament, but the world will rejoice; you will be sorrowful, but your sorrow will turn into joy. When a woman is in travail she has sorrow, because her hour has come; but when she is delivered of the child, she no longer remembers the anguish, for joy that a child is born into the world. So you have sorrow now, but I will see you again and your hearts will rejoice, and no one will take your joy from you. In that day you will ask nothing of me. Truly, truly, I say to you, if you ask anything of the Father, he will give it to you in my name. Hitherto you have asked nothing in my name; ask, and you will receive, that your joy may be full. . . . Jesus [said to his disciples,] "The hour is coming, indeed it has come, when you will be scattered, every man to his home, and will leave me alone; yet I am not alone, for the Father is with me. I have said this to you, that in me you may have peace. In the world you have tribulation; but be of good cheer, I have overcome the world."

—John 16:19-33

I hate to admit it, but I have difficulty with names. I think it's my age. I may start trying the technique another fellow used in the same situation. Whenever he met somebody he could not remember, he always asked, "Well, how's the old complaint?"

Everybody has an old complaint, you know. So when the man would ask about them, people thought he remembered who they were.

Consider for a moment the cartoon which showed a man standing in a bar. In a very reflective and somber mood he said to his drinking companion, "I come in here to drown my sorrows, but they've learned how to swim."

Those are two graphic pictures of life, aren't they? We all have those old complaints that hang on. We all have those sorrows that we can't drown, either with alcohol or with tears. Apart from our ongoing life struggles there are the different tragedies that strike us without warning. We identify with the word of Jesus, "In the world you have tribulation." *That's What the Man Said*; and we respond, "Yeah! Yeah, we know that!" ◇ **1.**

Fifteen or twenty years ago, Glenn Yarborough sang a song packed with pathos and carrying an image that describes so much of life. Written by Rod McKuen, the song begins, "How low is lonely? How deep is down?" While it is primarily a song about lost love, McKuen's lyrics speak to all the pain, and frustration, and brokenness we experience in life. His concluding question is a question each of us will ask ourselves at some dark time in our life: "Down, down, how deep is down?"

Maybe it's my age, but I don't hear popular music today that addresses the human issues as the lyrics of the songs fifteen or twenty-five years ago. The words are heart-gripping. Yes, Jesus, we believe you; "In the world you have tribulation." Let's look at what "tribulation" means to us today. The despair we hear in McKuen's song and the tribulation Jesus speaks of can take many forms.

How deep is down? It's as deep as that pain we feel as we sit beside the bed of a suffering child and can do nothing to help. The doctor is giving us little hope that she can help either. Down, down, how deep is down?

It's as deep as the pain of a broken heart as we stand at the casket of a loved one. Down, down, how deep is down?

It's as deep as the devastating emptiness we feel in relation to our children who have cut us off and won't let us enter their private world of feeling and thought. Down, down, how deep is down?

It's as deep and as throbbing as the gnawing loneliness of going to bed alone at night because our mate has walked out; the marriage is over. Down, down, how deep is down?

It's as deep as the frustration and helplessness of a young person who has just broken up with a steady sweetheart. Down, down, how deep is down?

It's as deep and as traumatic as a broken engagement to be married, just broken when the marriage was a month away. Down, down, how deep is down?

It's as deep as the impotence and anger we feel in ourselves when we've yielded to temptation, and the guilt beats at every corner of our mind as we storm out with Paul and rage at ourselves, "I do not do the good I want, but the evil I do not want is what I do" (Rom. 7:19).

That's how deep down is. ◇ **2.**

"In this world you have tribulation"—*That's What the Man Said*, and we can identify with him. Although maybe not as dramatic as down, down, the deepness of down, still the pressure of the everyday often comes off as tribulation. Perhaps you have heard of the salesman who was trying to sell a home freezer to a housewife. "You can save enough on food bills to pay for it," he said.

"Yes, I know," agreed the woman. "But you see, we're already paying for a compact car on the gasoline we save, a washing machine on the laundry bills we save, and a house on the rent we save. To tell you the truth, we just can't afford to save any more right now."

The pressure and the monotony of every day often come off as tribulation. Yes, Jesus, we hear you; and we know what you mean when you say, "In the world, you have tribulation."

But what else? Doesn't Jesus add something to that? "In the world, you have tribulation; but be of good cheer, for I have overcome the world." Yes! *That's What the Man Said.*

The question is, what are we going to do about accepting his promise, believing it, and being cheerful? First, we've got to know that the circumstances of our life are never as important as our attitudes toward those circumstances.

◇ **2.**

Read again the examples I listed of "how deep is down?" Put a check (☑) by those you have experienced, and an asterisk (*) by those experienced by some friend.

Here is a witness of that. Karabeth Sheleich lives in Harris Hill, New York. A member of the United Methodist church in Harris Hill, she was stricken with cerebral palsy as a child. She has to use crutches whether she is teaching her church class or leading a United Methodist Women's meeting. She also owns a store for needlepoint enthusiasts and is a fulltime mother to her two beautiful children. Karabeth is a woman who won't say, "I can't." Listen to her words from an article in the *United Methodist Reporter:* "I guess what makes me go is when someone says, 'It can't be done.' I decide with God's power I'm going to do it. Your attitude can handicap you as much as anything. I'd rather be here alive the way I am than not be here at all. God has given me life, and I want to glorify Him with my life as fully alive as it can be."

Doesn't that picture it? The circumstances of our life are never as important as our attitudes toward those circumstances.

◇ **3.**

◇ **3.**

Who is the person you know best who has shown that the circumstances of life are never as important as our attitudes toward those circumstances? Write a few sentences describing that person.

"In the world you have tribulation, but be of good cheer, I have overcome the world." *That's What the Man Said,* and because we believe him and accept his promise, we know that the circumstances of our life are never as important as our attitude toward those circumstances.

That suggests a second thing: *We must cease living our lives as a typographical error.* That's an image from the Danish philosopher-theologian Sören Kierkegaard. He said that persons exist like a typographical error that refuses to be erased.

You've seen people who live that way—determined to remain miserable for the whole of their life. They think they've been called to be living witness to the injustice that exists in this world, and they think that a big part of that injustice is focused on them.

You've seen some of those people, and you may have some of them as friends. (You may be one of those persons.) They may not verbalize it in specific words, but everything they say and do communicates their deepest self-understanding: "Poor me!"

It takes a lot of energy to live that way. Have you ever thought of it in that fashion? It's not easy to stay miserable all your life. You have to gather very carefully the evidence you're going to use to support your case. Mark Trotter, who suggested this idea to me, spoke about Kierkegaard's image:

> If you want to believe that "nobody knows the trouble I've seen," then don't read biographies, because if you do, you'll read about people who know what you've seen, and much worse.
>
> If you want to believe that you can't overcome whatever has come over you, then don't look around you, especially in church, because if you do, you'll see people who have faced worse and overcome it.
>
> If you want to believe, as many people in our time still want to believe, that this is a time of peril and danger, that it is the worst

possible time in which to live, then you can't read history because if you read history you're going to discover there were worse times.

The evidence for unhappiness is there. You can find it. But the other evidence is there, too. So you pretty much choose which argument you want to support.

Maybe Kierkegaard was right. Martyrdom is a protest against God. To choose to be perenially unhappy in this life is to get back at Him for what He's done to you. So if anybody suggests to you that this is a great life, all you need to do is offer yourself as a living testimony to the contrary.

That's not to suggest that misery isn't real in this world. It's not to minimize the pain you feel in your life. When something happens to you to crush your dreams, wound your heart, then you'd better be unhappy. Something is wrong with you if you're not. At such a time it is natural and healthy to raise questions, be angry, curse, to protest evil against God. You've had a terrible blow in your life, and you ought to be unhappy because of it. But one thing you have to decide: Are you going to spend the rest of your life collecting grievances for what has happened to you, or are you going to take God on his promise that life will always be good, no matter what happens? (Trotter, June 1, 1980)

Are you going to believe what Jesus said: "In this world you have tribulation, but be of good cheer, I have overcome the world." To live life as a typographical error is to believe the first part of what Jesus said and not go on to the second part.

Living life as a typographcal error—get that picture clearly in your mind. One day the sales manager of a large corporation was complaining to his secretary about one of his men. "Harry has such a bad memory," he said, "it's a wonder he remembers to breathe! Why, I asked him to pick up a newspaper on his way back from lunch, but I'm not sure he'll even remember his way back to the office!"

About that time, the door burst open. It was Harry, and he had an excited look on his face. "Guess what!" he exclaimed. "At lunch I ran into old man Jones, who hasn't given us an order in seven years. And you're not going to believe this. Before I left I talked him into a million-dollar contract. Can you believe that?"

The sales manager sighed rather disgustedly and turned to his secretary. "What did I tell you?" he said. "He forgot the newspaper!"

There are a lot of people in the world today just like that sales manager, aren't there? No matter what kind of wonderful thing happens to them, no matter what kind of wonderful situation they find themselves occupying, they still have a way of spotting what's wrong and focusing on it intently. They live as a typographical error that refuses to be erased. They won't forget the bad things. They won't allow the past to be the past. They always want to bring it into the present. They are intent on being martyrs. They don't seem to believe they deserve to be happy. They continually find causes to close their eyes to any reason there might be for enjoying life. They can accept a part of what Jesus said but not the whole.

"In the world you have tribulation; *but be of good cheer, I have overcome the world.*"

Let's make a leap in our thinking now which will enable others to make a leap in theirs. The best way to believe Jesus, and to make his truth real in our life, is to join Jesus in his continuing work of "overcoming the world." I'm reminded of another promise of Jesus, very much like this one. You'll find it in Matthew 11:28-30: "Come to me, all who labor and are heavy laden, and I will give you rest. Take my yoke upon you, and learn from me; for I am gentle and lowly in heart, and you will find rest for your souls. For my yoke is easy, and my burden is light."

What a beautiful promise, this promise of rest! But again, hear the second part of Jesus' statement because there is also a call to take up a burden. I believe those two calls are more closely linked than we have ever imagined. In a mysterious way that we will never understand, our burden is eased by helping bear the burdens of others. Tennyson said, "My idea of heaven is the perpetual ministry of one soul to another." That's a little radical, but I think at the heart of it is a great truth. How happy are those, how full of good cheer are those who join Jesus in overcoming the tribulation of the world.

Norman Neaves, pastor of the Church of the Servant in Oklahoma City, has told the story of a friend of his, David Brinker. David is an ophthamologist in Oklahoma City and a member of the Church of the Servant. He goes on medical eye missions twice a year to countries in Central and South America. He goes at his own expense to do surgeries and dispense glasses for some of the very poorest people in this hemisphere. Norman went to Dr. Brinker's office one day for an appointment. While waiting for that appointment, he noticed a little statement on the wall in which Dr. Brinker explains why he goes on those medical missions twice a year.

The first thing David said was this: "I have a talent which God has given me. Part is natural and part is learned. This talent has made me reasonably comfortable in life and now I can share this gift with others who would never otherwise receive it. Going on two missions a year is close to tithing his talent. I feel we're doing God's work, and I feel close to him while working on a mission."

Then Dr. Brinker wrote this: "There is a core of people on each mission who make me a better person just by being around them. They come from comfortable backgrounds, but without complaint they step into an environment of hardship, give overwhelming hours of work, and literally lay their hands on the poorest and dirtiest peoples of the world. They do this in the name of Jesus Christ. They are soft-spoken, patient, supportive people. I pray each time that I could become more like them."

Then David shared this little story as an example of why he goes on the missions:

> One day I received a patient, a lovely girl with two children and with [only] hand-motion vision. Examining her with the tools I had, I could find nothing wrong except that I couldn't focus on her retina at all. After dilating her and examining her retina with a special instrument, I recognized the signs of extreme myopia, and I told her she would need glasses. She exclaimed, *"No plata, no plata,"* which meant she couldn't pay for them. I told her we would, this very day, *give* her a pair of glasses. She began to cry, and all of the nurses in the clinic cried with her. She put on the glasses and walked over to her young son, whom she had never seen clearly before, and she began to cry again.

At the bottom of David's statement was this last one: "Grateful old patients and parents of patients frequently grasp my hand and mutter in Spanish, 'God will reward you.'" And to that Dr. Brinker simply wrote, "He already has!"

You see, the best way to believe Jesus and to make his truth real in your life is to join him in his continuing work of overcoming the world. In a mysterious way that we will never understand, our burden is eased by helping bear the burdens of others.   ◇ **4.**

I did most of the work on this chapter in Tom and Carol Iverson's beautiful home on Pickwick Lake in West Tennessee. It was one of those occasions when I went away for two or three days to be renewed and to have some concentrated study time.

My wife, Jerry, was with me. Not wanting to bother her with dictation on a tape recorder, I was working in Amy Iverson's bedroom. As I came to complete the dictation of this chapter, I looked over on the wall at a beautiful needlepoint that was framed. It was this message: "Today is the tomorrow that worried you yesterday, and all is well."

It is an appropriate response to Jesus' words: "In the world you have tribulation; but be of good cheer, I have overcome the world."

Jesus doesn't promise us that the tomorrows of our life will be free of tribulation. He does promise that he will be present with us. Because he has overcome the world, so can we—with his grace and strength.

◇ **4.**

The three truths that we have listed in response to this word of Jesus are:

1. The circumstances of our life are never as important as our attitudes toward those circumstances.

2. We must cease living our life as a typographical error.

3. The best way to believe Jesus and to make real his truth in our life is to join Jesus in his continuing work of "overcoming the world."

What changes must you make in your attitudes, actions, and/or lifestyle if you are to take these lessons seriously? It will help to put your answer in writing. Do so here.

CHAPTER ◇ 10

Living in Our Second Childhood

◇ **1.**

And they came to Capernaum; and when he was in the house he asked them, "What were you discussing on the way?" But they were silent; for on the way they had discussed with one another who was the greatest. And he sat down and called the twelve; and he said to them, "If any one would be first, he must be last of all and servant of all." And he took a child, and put him in the midst of them; and taking him in his arms, he said to them, "Whoever receives one such child in my name receives me; and whoever receives me, receives not me but him who sent me."

—Mark 9:33-37

Earl Loomis tells of a little boy who was sitting at a lunch counter with his mother and his older sister. After taking the mother's and sister's orders, the waitress addressed the little brother.

"What will you have, young man?"

"I'll order for him," said his sister.

Again the waitress asked the boy what he would have, and the mother said, "I'll order for him."

The waitress repeated, "Young man, what will you have?"

"A hamburger," the youngster said.

"Would you like rare, medium, or well done?"

"Well done, please," said the lad, brightening a bit.

"Would you like mustard, pickles, onions, relish, or catsup?"

In a burst of self-confidence the boy exclaimed, "The whole works!" As the waitress walked away, the lad said, "Gee, Mommy, she thinks I'm real!"

That's what little children might have said of Jesus. Parents were bringing their children to Jesus in order to be blessed. The disciples took strong decisive action, thinking that they needed to protect Jesus and his priorities. Teachings and miracles should preoccupy his time and attention, not the touching of children to satisfy a mother's whims.

Now, the disciples' motives may have been right, but certainly their feelings were wrong. They rebuked the parents and therefore showed the low value that they placed upon the person of a small child. Not only that, but, though they had been with Jesus for two years, they had not yet caught his spirit. Even his most recent words about receiving a little child as the way of receiving him and His Father did not get through to them. ◇ **1.**

So when Jesus noticed that they were scolding parents for bringing their children, he became angry. There are not many instances in scripture where it says that Jesus was angry. But he was angry because he knew that these disciples had not gotten his message. "Let the children come to me, do not hinder them, for to such belongs the kingdom of God" (Mark 10:14). *That's What the Man Said*. In saying that, he laid down the requirement for receiving and living in the kingdom. "Truly, . . . whoever does not receive the kingdom of God like a child shall not enter it" (Mark 10:15).   ◇ **2.**

Do you remember Nicodemus? We studied about him in chapter 3. Nicodemus came to Jesus inquiring what he should do to inherit eternal life. And to his elder, this venerable leader among the Jewish aristocracy, Jesus said the same thing that he said in our text: "You must be born again!" Nicodemus was puzzled; perturbed really. "I'm an old man," he said, "How can I be born again? I came here by night seeking you out. Don't give me riddles; I don't want double talk—give me a straight answer!"

But Jesus did not back down from his original dictum: "You must be born again. Truly, truly, I say to you, unless one is born anew, he cannot see the kingdom of God" (John 3:3). And Matthew quotes Jesus as saying the same thing in another context, "Unless you turn and become like children, you will never enter the kingdom of heaven (Matt. 18:3).   ◇ **3.**

In one of his sermons, the eminent theologian Paul Tillich paraphrased Jesus' words on this biblical text in this way: "The nature of salvation is the nature of a child."

There is a story about a neurotic business executive who finally took the time for a vacation. He sent a picture postcard to his psychiatrist with this message: "Having a good time! Wish you were here to tell me why." That man didn't need a psychiatrist; he needed to hear Jesus' words: "Whoever does not receive the kingdom of God like a child shall not enter it."

I've titled this chapter "Living in Our Second Childhood." Now, it's a good rule of thumb in teaching, preaching, and writing that we not use images that we have to explain. I'm breaking that rule in this instance because that image is precisely the one I want to use, yet it does need redemption from some common thoughts. We might say of a person in whom senility has begun to work, "She is living in her second childhood." We say it tenderly and with understanding affection. Or we might say of an elderly widower who is running after a woman thirty years his junior, "The old codger is trying to be a boy again. He's reverted to a second childhood." We say it judgmentally with at least a degree of anger, especially if he has divorced his wife or if we are friends of the wife he has recently lost in death.

When we use the term *second childhood*, more often than not we refer to something over which a person has no control. It just happens. It happens because of the loss of some of our faculties. That's my corrective word as I suggest the image today. Jesus is saying that receiving and living in the kingdom is *living in our*

◇ **2.**

And they were bringing children to him, that he might touch them; and the disciples rebuked them. But when Jesus saw it he was indignant, and said to them, "Let the children come to me, do not hinder them; for to such belongs the kingdom of God. Truly, I say to you, whoever does not receive the kingdom of God like a child shall not enter it." And he took them in his arms and blessed them, laying his hands upon them.
—Mark 10:13-16

◇ **3.**

At that time the disciples came to Jesus, saying, "Who is the greatest in the kingdom of heaven?" And calling to him a child, he put him in the midst of them, and said, "Truly, I say to you, unless you turn and become like children, you will never enter the kingdom of heaven. Whoever humbles himself like this child, he is the greatest in the kingdom of heaven.
—Matthew 18:1-4

◇ **4.**
Make a list of the characteristics of a child . . . all the characteristics as you think of them, good, bad, positive, negative. List them as one-word descriptions.

Now put a ☑ check by those characteristics you think Jesus was thinking about when he called us to childlikeness.

second childhood by deliberate choice. It's not the loss of faculties; it is deliberately *taking on,* appropriating, characteristics of "children of God."

First, faith to enter the kingdom is childlike. This is clear in Jesus' words: "Let the children come to me, do not hinder them; for to such belongs the kingdom of God."

Do you read Hank Ketcham's comic strip, *Dennis the Menace*? The Wilsons are Dennis's next-door neighbors. In one cartoon episode, Mrs. Wilson tells Dennis that Mr. Wilson was once just like him. Dennis explains to his friend that Mr. Wilson got dirty, and had fights, and stole cookies, and broke things, etc., just the way Dennis did. To which his friend replies: "Gee! He sounds like a reg'lar fella! I wonder where he went wrong?"

That's what Jesus might ask of us. "Where did you go wrong?" That's what he was saying to his disciples: "Fellows, you've got it all wrong—arguing about the chief seats in the kingdom! You've missed the point! You're headed in the wrong direction! Unless you turn and become as children, you will not enter the kingdom."

Faith to enter the kingdom is childlike, because children have the capacity to trust. If we became more like a child, we would be more graceful—that is, full of God's grace—because we would be more trusting; we would be more accepting of God's grace. Tillich's paraphrase of Jesus' words, which I quoted earlier, affirms this idea: "The nature of salvation is the nature of a child." Children are joyful and grateful, and they receive openly without asking a lot of questions.

One of our problems as parents is that we give our children everything but the one thing that really matters. John Thompson writes in *Pulpit Digest*: "We give them all kinds of electronic games, the latest style of clothes, but we do not give them the Kingdom of God. We cannot lead them to the Kingdom, because we have not entered ourselves. We're still trying to take the Kingdom by storm, rather than receiving it as grace. We do not humble ourselves as a child."

We'll never make it that way. To receive the kingdom requires childlike faith.   ◇ **4.**

So much for receiving the kingdom. What about living in it, about living in our second childhood? What are some of the marks?

1. Having the capacity to wonder
2. Being capable of spontaneity
3. Being comfortable with self
4. Being committed to change

Let's look briefly at these. First, having the capacity to

wonder. John Killinger has written so graphically about this aspect of children.

> Children are naturally curious and want answers to many things; they are often satisfied with the simplest of explanations. "What makes the leaves turn red and gold in the autumn?" they want to know. "A little fellow named Jack Frost paints them," we say. "When does he paint them?" they ask. "Before you get up in the morning," we reply. And they are delighted. It isn't that they fully accept the answer; their young minds are already questioning such fanciful responses. But they like it. They see the universe as music and poetry. Jack Frost or photosynthesis, it is the same. A world of wonder.
>
> The books they enjoy are a clue to this. *Alice in Wonderland, The Wizard of Oz, Dr. Seuss.* A world of fantasy and make-believe, where rabbits talk and robots can earn a real heart and Grinches can indeed steal Christmas.
>
> It isn't that they don't understand the real world. They do. They understand it better than grownups, because they see it whole, with the ego and the id together. They haven't compartmentalized it and rationalized it and turned it into a spare-parts factory. They accept their environment as miraculous, and don't relegate God to a book and an ancient history. For them, Jesus can still turn water into wine and make a blind man see and raise the dead to life. For them, the world is still mystery and life is grace. They can see God in a puddle of water or the glow of a firefly. . . . Oh, they would have a difficult time organizing the world without us, it is true. They need the adults to keep a roof over their heads and cut their meat and make them eat their spinach. But how much poorer we would be without their vision, their way of seeing things. We need their point of view, said Jesus, to enter the Kingdom.
> (Killinger, pp. 56-57)   ◇ **5.**

So, children have a capacity to wonder. They are also *capable of spontaneity*. That's the second mark of a child that we need in order to live in our second childhood as children of the kingdom.

We need that, the willingness and ability to act or go at once on what one sees, hears, or comes to understand. Spontaneity is not strangled in a young child by careful calculation and cautious skepticism. Jesus always seemed to live this way before God, and he encouraged the spontaneous impulse in others. Here it is in a picture.

> She came into the kitchen
> Where we were drinking tea.
> Nearly four, she banged the door
> And said, "Can God see me?"
>
> Her father lowered his cup and smiled;
> his eyes caught mine.
> He said, "Yes, of course, God sees you
>   all day and when you're in bed."

◇ **5.**
Go to your list of characteristics of children. Put an asterisk (*) by those characteristics that harmonize with having the capacity to wonder.

◇ **6.**

Go back to your list of characteristics of children. Underscore those characteristics that suggest spontaneity.

Wonder and spontaneity are twins, though not identical. We are not likely to have the capacity to wonder without being capable of spontancity.

Reflect on your own life. Write a few sentences about your reservations concerning wonder and spontaneity or about how you feel limited in your ability to wonder and be spontaneous.

She fingered her new skipping rope,
handle dangling
    on the floor,
Then slowly wound it 'round her hands
And walked back out the door.

Then down the garden path she ran,
her small black boots
    light tripping
We saw her face light up with joy.
"Look, God!" she cried. "I'm skipping."

It's a great day in all of our lives when we come to that point, the point of feeling so good about ourselves and so free and spontaneous that we can let God know about it.

Callerin, the French statesman, once said profoundly but cynically, "Distrust first impulses; they are nearly always right." How true! And yet, too many of us have trained ourselves to check childlike spontaneity. So we've become carefully calculating. We calculate the money we give to God, we calculate as to whether we're going to respond to that call for help. We calculate how we're going to relate to others. We teach our children to hold back. How often do we say, "You better look before you leap." We might need to change that, on some occasions at least to "Don't look before you leap. If you do, you will decide to sit down."

Again, too many of us have become too calculating, too skeptical; and so, we've done too little leaping in faith. We need to recover that childlike capacity for spontaneity.   ◇ **6.**

Now, the third mark of a child that we need: children are comfortable with self.

I know that it is in childhood that feelings about one's self are determined. I know that if self-esteem is not fostered in children, they are in for trouble later on. Nothing is more important in parenting than to pay attention to your child's feelings about himself or herself.

Yet, until adults and life experiences distort it, children are usually comfortable with themselves. Even if we have lost that—which we normally do—life in the kingdom requires that we recover it. Until we teach them otherwise, children don't count their talents or concern themselves with dazzling the world.

To be comfortable with ourselves is one of the marks of humility. Jesus put being humble and being childlike together. "Whoever humbles himself like this child, he is the greatest in the kingdom of heaven." To be comfortable with ourselves is to be humble. To be humble is to know who we are, to know who we are in our *strength* and in our *weakness*.

Too often we associate humility with weakness. It is precisely the opposite. The humble know their weakness, but knowing our weakness becomes a source of strength. Sir Isaac Newton was a good example of humility. A fellow scientist talked about him in this way:

> The modesty of Sir Isaac Newton, in reference to his great discoveries, was not founded on any indifference to the fame which they conferred, or upon any erroneous judgment of their importance to science. The whole of his life proves that he knew his place as a philosopher, and was determined to assert and vindicate his rights. His modesty arose from the depth and extent of his knowledge, which showed him what a small portion of nature he had been able to examine, and how much remained to be explored in the same field in which he had himself labored. In the magnitude of the comparison he recognized his own littleness; and a short time before his death he uttered this memorable sentiment: "I do not know what I may appear to the world, but to myself I seem to have been only like a boy playing on the seashore, and diverting myself in now and then finding a smoother pebble or a prettier shell than ordinary, whilst the great ocean of truth lay all undiscovered before me." (Fosdick, *On Being Fit to Live With*, pp. 147-148)

Newton was a great man with a brilliant mind, but he was humble. He knew his strength and weakness. He was comfortable with himself.   ◇ **7.**

One of the most telling symbols of our day is seen in the athletic arenas of our nation—crowds of fans and entire athletic teams reaching toward heaven their raised forefinger and piercing the air with their in-unison roar, "We're number one!"

It may or may not be true, but it is the plaintive cry of humankind, going all the way back to Adam and Eve in the garden; picked up by Jesus' disciples, James and John, who requested chief seats in the kingdom; and grasped for, to some degree, by all of us. In fact, the desire to be number one may be our original sin.

The world's view is so different from Jesus' view. "Become humble," he said, "as a little child." To be kingdom people calls for a deliberate decision to enter our second childhood, which includes being comfortable with ourselves.   ◇ **8.**

I can't forget that marvelous story Bishop Earl Hunt tells about a visit with Mary Culler White. Miss White had served for years as a missionary in China. Bishop Hunt went to call on her when she was ninety-five and living in the Brooks-Howell home in Asheville, North Carolina. When he was about to conclude his visit, she offered this prayer for the bishop: "Now, Lord, thou knowest that Earl has come to see me, and thou knowest that he is a bishop. But thou art always aware that this doesn't mean a thing in the world to me."

This is the only way the kingdom can expand—the only way the church grows and serves—when people who are living in their second childhood feel comfortable with who they are and know they are needed and that they count—no matter how many talents they have or who they are.

◇ **7.**
Get a picture in your mind of a particular person you consider *humble*. Think about that person—his/her attitudes, actions, values, and relationships (how he or she relates to others). Does the person know herself? Is he comfortable with himself? What about awareness of strength and weakness? Make some notes about that person.

How does looking at the person help you in being comfortable with yourself?

◇ **8.**
Go back to your list of characteristics of a child. Select the characteristics that would harmonize with the notion of being comfortable with ourselves, of being humble, and list them here.

◇ **9.**
Go back to your list of characteristics of a child. Are there any characteristics left that have not been starred or underlined that might harmonize with a willingness to change? Underline them.

Now check the ones you originally checked as being characteristics Jesus might have been thinking about when he called us to be kingdom children. Are any of them not included in what we have talked about in our study? If so, reflect more about them.

Now, a final characteristic of children that we need to appropriate in order to live in our second childhood as children of the kingdom is a commitment to change. What this commitment really means is to be teachable. And children are that. They are teachable; they are open, and Jesus calls us to that.

The early Christian believers called themselves "followers of the Way." Isn't that an apt description? They knew they had not arrived. They realized they had much more to discover and larger answers to live into. That must be the set of our soul, the stance of our life—to be open, teachable, reachable. ◇ **9.**

This calls us back to Matthew's record of Jesus' word: "Unless you are converted and become as little children, you will by no means enter the kingdom of heaven" (18:3, NKJV). The Revised Standard Version has it "unless you turn." The notion is a willingness to change direction. To repent and be converted is to turn back in humility as a child, to open ourselves in childlike humility to be changed by Christ. To be converted is to willingly place ourselves in humble relationship with Jesus Christ.

Conversion may be a one-time event. In fact, there should be that time in our life when it all comes to focus and we make that trusting commitment to Jesus Christ, accepting his grace for salvation. But living in our second childhood as kingdom children means living a conversion-style life, in which we are always open to change.

And change comes—always. All sorts of changes, like that which came to Martin Sheen, the actor. He tells his story in an interview with Steven Saint printed in the *National Catholic Reporter*. He was raised a good Catholic, but then got caught up in the business of living sumptuously, making a name, surrounding himself with all the extravagances of the ultimate consumer. Then one day in 1977, he was in the Philippines, making the movie, *Apocalypse Now*. He had a heart attack. "I began to examine my life," he said, "what I was doing with it, exploring many ideas. I went to all parts of the world in search of something. I don't know what it was I was looking for, but I was looking for something." That journey ended in 1981, in India, making another movie, *Gandhi*.

> One day we were driving somewhere and these children came up and were hanging on the back of the taxicab. I looked out and saw their faces. These malnourished children looked like old people. Their teeth were gone. Bugs were in their hair. And I suddenly knew what I had to do. We stopped the car. We got them inside, and I said, "Whoever they are and whatever they are doing, they are doing it now with me. They are my children this day." And I was able to hold those children. And as I held them, I was able to see my children (Saint, p. 9).

Martin Sheen was converted. Children had made him a child, and he entered his second childhood. Willingness to change is characteristic of kingdom children without respect for age.

"Whoever does not receive the kingdom of God like a child shall not enter it." *That's What the Man Said* and still says as he calls us to live in our second childhood; that is, to have the capacity to wonder, to be capable of spontaneity, to be comfortable with self, and to be committed to change. ◇ **10.**

◇ **10.**
Spend some time recalling and reflecting upon two occasions or events in your life: First, when you first trusted Christ for salvation, what you might refer to as your conversion or your faith commitment, to Christ as your Savior.

Second, another conversion in your life, the most recent—a time when you made a specific change—maybe not as dramatic but something like what happened to Martin Sheen.

CHAPTER ◇ 11

Cross-bearing Discipleship

◇ 1.

He said to all, "If any man would come after me, let him deny himself and take up his cross daily and follow me. For whoever would save his life will lose it; and whoever loses his life for my sake, he will save it. For what does it profit a man if he gains the whole world and loses or forfeits himself? For whoever is ashamed of me and of my words, of him will the Son of man be ashamed when he comes in his glory and the glory of the Father and of the holy angels. But I tell you truly, there are some standing here who will not taste death before they see the kingdom of God."

—Luke 9:23-27

The opening sentence of Scott Peck's popular book *The Road Less Traveled* is a prosaic but marvelous one. Now I know those two words don't fit well together, *prosaic* and *marvelous*. But in this instance they do. The sentence? Just three words: "Life is difficult."

It would be prosaic, even irresponsible, to make this statement in response to someone who has just poured out his or her soul to us, anguishing over burdens, sharing a hurting heart. "Well, life is difficult, you know," would be a prosaic witness of an unwillingness to try to get into the skin of another, to feel with the other, to share the throbbing of another's soul.

But here in Peck it's a wonderful sentence because it's the beginning of a book about life, and what could be more descriptive? Life is difficult, and the sentence certainly fits well with the book's title, *The Road Less Traveled*.

We might appropriately introduce this chapter with the words: "Life is difficult." In his book, Peck goes on to say that although this is one of the greatest truths, most of us don't see it. Instead, we "moan more or less incessantly, noisily or subtly, about the enormity of [our] problems," as if life is supposed to be easy for us, but that what has happened to us now has never happened to anybody else before—at least not in the excruciating painful or insoluble way that it has burdened us.

A cartoon showed a huge desk and an executive sitting behind it. He is obviously the CEO of some company. Standing meekly on the other side of the desk is another man dressed in work clothes, obviously a menial worker in the organization. The man says to the boss, "If it's any comfort, it's lonely at the bottom, too."

Life is difficult for everybody. But Jesus goes even further than that, and the phrase "life is difficult," really sounds prosaic up against his word: "If any man would come after me, let him deny himself and take up his cross daily and follow me." *That's What the Man Said*, and that's what we're going to look at in this chapter.

◇ 1.

Herbert Farmer has been one of the most convincing inter-preters of the Christian way in this century. In his book *God and Men*, he shared this personal experience:

> Many years ago as a young man I was speaking on the love of God; there was in the congregation an old Polish Jew who had been convert-ed to the Christian faith. He came to me afterward and said: "You have no right to speak of the love of God, until you have seen, as I have seen, a massacre of Jews in Poland—until you have seen, as I have seen, the blood of your dearest friends running in the gutters on a gray winter morning." I asked him later how it was that having seen such a massacre, he had come to believe in the love of God. The answer he gave in effect was that the Christian gospel first began to lay hold of him because it bade him see God—the love of God—as it were, just where he was, just where he could not but always be in his thoughts and memories—in those bloodstained streets on that gray morning. [Thus he saw] the love of God—not somewhere else—but in the midst of just that sort of thing, in the blood and agony of Calvary. He did at least know, he said, that this was a message that grappled with the facts, and then he went on to say something the sense of which I shall always remember though the words I have forgotten. He said, "As I looked at that man upon the Cross . . . it was at a point of final crisis and decision in my life; I knew I must make up my mind once and for all, and either take my stand beside him and share in his undefeated faith in God . . . or else fall finally into a bottomless pit of bitterness, hatred, and unutterable despair. (Farmer, pp. 190-191)   ◇ **2.**

So, these words of Jesus are a call to decision: "If any man would come after me, let him deny himself and take up his cross daily and follow me."

Someone has said that the number of new things we need to learn is small compared with the number of old things we need to be reminded of. So, rather than try to state them in any new way or grab your attention by imaginative rewording, let's confront head-on precisely what Jesus said. He said, first, to deny self; second, to take up your cross; and third, to follow him.

Even the severest critics of Jesus would never accuse him of beating around the bush. He always spoke directly, frankly, yet ever so tenderly. Never was he more explicit than here at Caesarea when he presented the demands of discipleship. The setting of this text in Mark's Gospel follows the revealing testimony of Peter at Caesarea Philippi (8:27-33). The disciples had been amazingly blind to who Jesus was. Their minds were so clouded that they didn't even get the message of the feeding of the multitude; now they had also wit-nessed the healing of a blind man, and Jesus confronted them with the question: "Who am I?" Peter gives that magnificent statement of faith, "Thou art the Christ" (Mark 8:29, KJV). *Cristos* in the Greek is the equivalent of the Hebrew *messiah*. So, Peter speaks for the disciples, confessing Jesus as the Messiah.

◇ **2.**
Think back upon your life. What is your most memorable encounter with the Cross, the occasion when Jesus hanging on a cross impacted your life? Describe that experience.

Again, while the disciples know that Jesus is God's Messiah and his mission is to be deliverance and salvation, they are still limited in their knowledge as to who the Messiah really is. So Jesus begins to teach them. He was the Messiah, but such a Messiah as no Jew had ever perceived.

How shocked they must have been when he proceeded to tell them, "The Son of Man must suffer many things . . . and be killed, and after three days rise again." Those words were so shocking that Peter rebuked Jesus for speaking in such a fashion. And Jesus then identified Peter with Satan, saying to him, in what must have been as much anger as we have ever seen in Jesus: "Get thee behind me, Satan! For you are not on the side of God, but of men."

Could Peter's challenge of Jesus have caused a flashback to the wilderness experience in which Satan had tried to convince Jesus to give up the way of the cross? Here the temptation is veiled in the caring love of a close friend. But Jesus is so certain that he doesn't even take time to discuss the issue. He rebukes Peter for being a stooge of Satan, seeking to divert Jesus from his messianic destiny under God.

Jesus used a strong word. He began to teach them that the Son of man must suffer. Jesus saw it as the divine necessity. God's will for him determined the way, and the way was that of suffering and death.

So, it was after revealing clearly who he was that Jesus gave us directions for discipleship: "If any man would come after me, let him deny himself and take up his cross daily and follow me." *That's What the Man Said*, so let's move through that call and find its meaning for us.

First, *deny yourself.*   ◇ **3.**

Self-denial means "to make yourself a stranger to yourself." It indicates that your own wishes should mean nothing to you if they contradict God's will. It affirms simply for the Christian that any way but God's way is wrong. Jesus knew this. He was able to overcome the tempter because during days and nights in the wilderness he found strength through surrender to God. When the crowds, impressed by his miracles, sought to make him king, he went into the hills. Here he found guidance for the future through the power of submission to the Father. Even at the end there was no lack of courage at Calvary because of the bravery of obedience in Gethsemane.

> Self-denial or self-yielding to God is no mere sideline. It is indispensable to Christian living and vital to every spiritual experience. Hear the Master speak: "Whoever would save his life will lose it, and whoever loses his life for my sake will find it."
>
> Unsurrendered self, or selfishness, blinds us to that which is

◇ **3.**
Before you read further, spend a few minutes reflecting on self-denial. What does Jesus' call to *deny self* mean to you?

essential. Self-gratification says, "I want what I want"; self-denial says, "I want what I need." The selfish man wants his pocketbook full; the surrendered man desires treasures that neither moth nor rust consumes.

Selfishness says, "Me, my, mine"; selflessness says, "You, yours, theirs." The results may deceive us, for the fruits of want and wealth and possession and seizure are nearly always evident and tangible. On the other hand, the rewards of the consecrated self are often intangible and unseen. There was the rich farmer. So interested was he in his barns and grain and goods that the thing of foremost importance was forgotten. Consider the rich young man. His eyes were so fixed on what he had that he rejected that supreme "one thing." (Wallace D. Chappell, pp. 22-23)

Now I'm aware of the fact that we have perverted this exhortation of Jesus. Jesus is calling us not to self-depreciation but to self-fulfillment. Jesus knew, as modern psychologists are beginning to learn, that life is found only by getting outside ourselves. Most of our problems are not because we don't think enough of ourselves but because our self is all we think about.

I like Leo Buscaglia, that marvelously off-beat psychologist who teaches classes in love at the University of Southern California. He has written some wonderful books; in all of those books he emphasizes the paradox of giving in order to receive, denying ourselves in order to be fulfilled. In *Living, Loving and Learning*, Buscaglia identifies one thing that he considers "voluntarily mandatory" and that is that "everybody do something for somebody else." When one of his students, Joel, asked "What's there to do?"—Buscaglia took him to a convalescent home not far from the USC campus. Inside were a lot of aged people lying around on beds in cotton gowns, just staring at the ceiling. They walked into the hospital, and Joel said, "What'll I do here? I don't know anything about gerontology." And Buscaglia said, "Good. You see that lady over there? Go over and say hello."

"That's all?" "That's all."

So Joel went over to the lady and said, "Hello." She looked at him suspiciously and then asked, "Are you a relative?" Joel said, "No."

"Good," she said, "sit down."

So he sat down and they started to talk. I'm going to use Buscaglia's words now, because I want you to hear them as he wrote them.

O, my goodness, the things she told him! . . . This woman had known so many wondrous things about life, about love, about pain, about suffering. Even about approaching death, with which she had to make some kind of peace. But no one cared about listening! [Joel] started going once a week, and pretty soon that day began to be known as "Joel's day.". . . And probably the greatest triumphant mo-

◇ **4.**

Can you think of some experience in your life when meaning came because you willingly gave yourself, *at some cost*, to another or others? Describe that experience here. If you have not had such an experience, reflect on what that means.

ment in my educational career came one day when I walked out on campus and there was Joel, like the Pied Piper, with about thirty little old people following him, hobbling to a football game! (Buscaglia, pp. 215-216)

Isn't that a picture of finding life by losing life? We could see it everywhere if we would just open our eyes. No, let me say that differently. We can see it everywhere when the gospel opens our eyes. It's simply the way things are. We find life by losing life. So Jesus said, "Deny yourself." ◇ **4.**

"If any man would come after me, let him deny himself and take up his cross. . . ." *That's What the Man Said*—"Take up your cross."

The train from Evanston to Chicago used to pass a cemetery called Calvary. Since people went there only occasionally, the train stopped only on signal. As the train neared the cemetery, the conductor would call out: "The next station is Calvary. Is there anyone for Calvary?"

Here we have a parable of the train of life. It stops regularly to discharge passengers for the marketplace, the beauty salon, the amusement center, and other stations of popular appeal. But Calvary requires a definite request if we choose it as our destination. . . .

To experience the saving benefits of the Cross, we must know the glory of bearing it ourselves.

We have given the name of "cross" to many things that really are not crosses in the Christian sense of the word. Our misunderstanding of the meaning of the word *cross* is sometimes amusing, occasionally pathetic, and often silly. Many times, normal, average Christians, not seriously hurt by life, complain of poor teeth, of baldness, or of being overweight, as a "cross" they must bear. A woman married to a lazy, shiftless husband sighs that he is her "cross." How silly! These really are not crosses.

There are people who speak of poor health as a "cross" they must carry. Chronic illness, indeed, is a misfortune, but it is not a cross. Others speak of a calamity as a "cross." A calamity, such as an explosion, a fire, or a severe automobile accident may be a tragedy, but it is not a cross. Still others speak of sorrow as a "cross." The loss of a loved one, and the loneliness that follows, is a heartbreaking experience, but, again, it is not a cross. Each of these may be a heavy burden, but none of them is a cross. They are the misfortune and suffering of all humanity. Christian or not, all are heir to them. They are the sorrows and difficulties that all men share in common. "Taking up our cross" is not enduring courageously or stoically our misfortune. These are great virtues, to be sure, but Christianity is something other than physical courage or modern stoicism. (Woodson, pp. 32-33)

Calvary involves a personal choice—a choice to take up our cross.

Many years ago now John Watson wrote: "The Cross has been taken out of Jesus' hands and smothered with flowers; it has become what he would have hated, a source of graceful ideas and agreeable emotions. When Jesus presented the Cross to his disciples, he was certainly not thinking of a sentiment which can disturb no man's life nor redeem any man's soul, but of . . . the jagged nails which must pierce his soul."

When Jesus calls us to take up our cross, he means that we are to deliberately take upon ourselves a burden—a burden we would not take at all except by compulsion of God's love. Bearing our cross means carrying part of the terrible load of suffering and sin that God always carries because of love for humankind. It is volunteering our life to help heal the wounds of the world and to bridge the gap between God and humanity. It is the additional suffering we take upon ourselves, so that the suffering and woes of the world may be lessened and the life of others redeemed.   ◇ **5.**

◇ **5.**
Think of the Cross as *deliberately taking upon ourselves a burden we would not take except by the compulsion of God's love*. Now spend a few minutes thinking about how you are living, or refusing to live, a Cross-style life.

I think of Albert Schweitzer here. He awakened one morning with the realization that he could not accept life's happiness as a matter of course. He decided that he must give something of himself in return for the many advantages he enjoyed. So he gave up a successful life in Europe as a scholar and musician to become a medical doctor among the people of central Africa. As one of his biographers Hermann Hagedorn writes in *Prophet of the Wilderness:* "He had heard of the wretchedness of the jungle peoples, the native diseases and the plagues brought by European slave-dealers. . . . What a burden of debt lay on the white man, lay on himself, Albert Schweitzer, as one of the guilty race! He must repay what he could of his share by using the white man's science to alleviate the black man's pain. He would repay—with his life."

That's what taking up our cross means: deliberately choosing something that could be avoided. We choose to deny ourselves, to give ourselves without reservation in the service of Christ, to be a force of love for the sake of God's kingdom.

That leads to the next part of Jesus' call: "If any man would come after me, let him deny himself and take up his cross daily and follow me. *That's What the Man Said*—"Follow me."

Jesus was calling his disciples (and us) to carry on when He was no longer with them what he had begun. What he had begun was a ministry of renewing the world through love. If we're going to follow Jesus, we're to follow him in compassionate ministry. That ministry may take us into areas of our city where we don't want to go. It may put us with people with whom we are not comfortable. It may call us to tasks we will not choose ourselves.

I don't know anyone who writes of this with such clarity and pungent images as Clarence Jordan. You may know him from his paraphrase of the New Testament called *Cotton Patch Versions*. He was a committed Christian with a transparent balance of deep personal piety and courageous action expressing compassionate concern. Talking about following Jesus, he wrote:

◇ **6.**

And he came to Nazareth, where he had been brought up; and he went to the synagogue, as his custom was, on the sabbath day. And he stood up to read; and there was given to him the book of the prophet Isaiah. He opened the book and found the place where it was written, "The Spirit of the Lord is upon me, because he has anointed me to preach the good news to the poor. He has sent me to proclaim release to the captives and recovering of sight to the blind, to set at liberty those who are oppressed, to proclaim the acceptable year of the Lord."

And he closed the book, and gave it back to the attendant, and sat down; and the eyes of all in the synagogue were fixed on him. And he began to say to them, "Today this scripture has been fulfilled in your hearing."

—Luke 4:16-21

◇ **7.**

What changes in attitudes, habits, actions, and/or lifestyle are required of you if you take this call of Jesus seriously? Make some notes to which you might return in the future for a checkup if you choose cross-bearing discipleship.

[God] raised Jesus not as an invitation to us to come to heaven when we die, but as a declaration that He himself has now established permanent residence on earth. . . . The good news of the resurrection of Jesus is not that we shall die and go home with him, but that he has risen and comes home with us, bringing all his hungry, naked, thirsty, sick, prisoner brothers with him.

And we say, "Jesus, we'd be glad to have *you*, but all these motley brothers of yours, you had better send them home. *You* come in and we'll have some fried chicken. But you get your sick, naked, cold brothers out of here. We don't want them getting our new rug all messed up." (Jordan, p. 28)

The call to follow Jesus is the call to carry on what he began—feeding the hungry, clothing the naked, visiting prisons, giving cups of cold water in his name—doing "unto the least of these." ◇ **6.**

His ministry was that of renewing the world through love, and he has committed that ministry to us. *That's What the Man Said:* "If any man would come after me, let him deny himself and take up his cross daily and follow me." ◇ **7.**

CHAPTER ◇ 12

Not Everyone Who Says, "Lord, Lord"

Jesus came into Jerusalem, riding on a borrowed donkey. The crowds were beside themselves. They pulled off their coats and put them in the path, cut branches from the palm trees and spread them along the way. They began to shout out as they raised their hands in joyous exultation—"Hosannah to the Son of David! Hosannah in the highest!"

In his translation of the story, J. B. Philips puts it this way: "As he entered Jerusalem a shock ran through the whole city." "Who is this?" men cried. "This is Jesus, the prophet," replied the crowd, "the man from Nazareth in Galilee" (Matt. 21:10-11). ◇ **1.**

It was the welcoming of the Messiah. What a day! Festival, excitement—everything connected with a great event and a great parade.

But it ended almost immediately. Jesus ran the money changers out of the temple, got tangled up with a Pharisee because his teaching threatened the religious establishment, and confused his own disciples and set them on edge. Only a few days later, those who had shouted, "Hosannah!" were screaming, "Crucify him!"

But this was no surprise to Jesus. He expected it much earlier. He spoke to the "Hosannah/Crucify him" crowd at the beginning of his ministry in the Sermon on the Mount: "Not every one who says to me, 'Lord, Lord,' shall enter the kingdom of heaven, but [only] he who does the will of my Father who is in heaven" (Matt. 7:21). ◇ **2.**

That's What the Man Said, and it's a word we need to remember. It is a cryptic word which challenges our halfhearted response to Jesus and defines discipleship.

To appropriate Jesus' word, we need first to underscore the fact that Jesus didn't say that we shouldn't say, "Lord, Lord." Indeed, that is the only appropriate thing to say in the presence of Jesus.

One of the big problems we have with our understanding of and commitment to the Christian faith is precisely at this point.

◇ **1.**

The disciples went and did as Jesus had directed them; they brought the ass and the colt, and put their garments on them, and he sat thereon. Most of the crowd spread their garments on the road, and others cut branches from the trees and spread them on the road.

And the crowds that went before him and that followed him shouted, "Hosanna to the Son of David! Blessed is he who comes in the name of the Lord! Hosanna in the highest!" And when he entered into Jerusalem, all the city was stirred, saying, "Who is this?" And the crowds said, "This is the prophet Jesus from Nazareth of Galilee."

—Matthew 21:6-11

◇ **2.**

"Not every one who says to me, "Lord, Lord," shall enter the kingdom of heaven, but he who does the will of my Father who is in heaven. On that day many will say to me, "Lord, Lord, did we not prophesy in your name, and cast out demons in your name, and do many mighty works in your name?" And then will I declare to them, "I never knew you; depart from me, you evildoers."

—Matthew 7:21-23

Jesus wants to be our Savior—and many of us are very responsive to that possibility. But Jesus also wants to be our Lord—and not many of us are very open to that possibility. So let's nail down a truth which is a foundation truth of the Christian faith: Our Christian experience is to be personal but not private.

The theme of chapter 3 was "God Has No Grandchildren." In that chapter, I talked about William Gibson in his autobiographical *Mass for the Dead*, relating how after his mother's death he yearned for the faith that had strengthened her during her remarkable life—the faith that had upheld her during her courageous dying. So he took his mother's gold-rimmed glasses and her faded and well-worn prayerbook and sat in her favorite chair. He opened the prayerbook because he wanted to see what she had seen. He sat in her place of prayer and devotion because he wanted to feel what she had felt, to experience what had so deeply centered and empowered her, but nothing happened. It did not work. It never does!

We cannot claim another person's faith for our own. God has no grandchildren. Ours must be a personal faith; but—and this is the main point I'm making here—though it must be personal, it is not private.

The scriptures are clear about the whole matter. Individual experiences of God's presence are celebrated with great joy, but persons who have that experience are called "to do justice, and to love kindness, and to walk humbly with your God" (Mic. 6:8).

The apostle Paul underscored it in his comments to the Christians at Corinth. He rejoiced with the believers in their personal ecstasies and endorsed their desire for spiritual gifts. However, he makes it plain that firsthand spiritual awareness must connect with and lead to "the common good of all people and the upbuilding of the whole church."

The Christian experience is always personal but never private. ◇ **3.**

Christian piety is not a piety turned in on itself, not a religious experience of spiritual narcissism, always intent on reading one's own spiritual pulse—but a piety that leads to moral righteousness and to concern for other persons.

Christianity is always personal but never private. "Not every one who says to me, 'Lord, Lord,' shall enter the kingdom of heaven, but he who does the will of my Father who is in heaven."

I can't help but think of the electronic church here. The Oral Roberts death threat for money, the Jimmy and Tammy Bakker scandal, and the fall of Jimmy Swaggart raise questions about the integrity of the electronic church in the minds of a lot of people. There is a larger question than the question that has been raised in these three different incidents, and especially the personal moral questions related to the Bakkers and to Mr. Swaggart. The larger question concerns the purpose of the electronic church and the

◇ **3.**
Before you read on, ponder for a few minutes the difference between private and personal religious experience.

direction it takes. I think it raises the whole issue of the nature of the church.

Let me draw a comparison to illustrate. Culver Nelson in his sermon "Electronic Religion" reports that there are one million members in his denomination, Congregational, and 6,500 churches. The total budgets of all the congregations amount to about $350 million. That's almost exactly the same amount that the nine most prominent media ministries spend each year. Nelson has reminded us, however, that those nine media ministries support just three churches, five schools, and one hospital, among them all. But this small denomination has founded nearly 50 colleges and 15 theological seminaries and supports 85 homes for the aging, 6 homes for the disabled, 13 centers for alleviating poverty, 25 hospitals, and 3 children's homes. In addition it has 426 persons in chaplaincy or missionary work, serving overseas schools and hospitals in settlement houses and churches (Nelson, p. 439).

Note the difference. It is the very nature of the Christian faith that people gather for the worship of God and the service of the human community, that Christians engage in the kind of ministry that seeks to shape the character of human life and human experience. One wonders how the electronic church fits into the whole scheme of God's kingdom ideal on earth.   ◇ **4.**

"Not every one who says to me, 'Lord, Lord,' shall enter the kingdom of heaven, but he who does the will of my Father who is in heaven." *That's What the Man Said*, and it means at least this: that the Christian experience is personal but never private.

Remember, Jesus didn't say that we shouldn't say, "Lord, Lord," yet he did say that it wasn't enough to say, "Lord, Lord." *Our life must reflect what we affirm.* That's the second thing I want us to underscore. *Our life must reflect what we affirm.*

Jesus is addressing the problem of glib language. It was rather easy in the excitement and joy of that first Palm Sunday for the people to shout out "Hosanna . . .! Blessed is he who comes in the name of the Lord!" But those turned out to be glib words when we see what those same people were doing a few days later—calling for the crucifixion of this one whom they had a few days before acclaimed.

You see, our language reflects what we believe, what we really think is important, and what we hold most dear. But the main point here is that our life should reflect what we affirm. Not only our words but also our deeds can take God's name in vain. *That's What the Man Said:* "Not every one who says to me, 'Lord, Lord' shall enter the kingdom of heaven, but he who does the will of my Father who is in heaven."

That we don't have to speak to violate the third commandment is a troubling thought, isn't it? "You shall not take the name of the Lord your God in vain; for the Lord will not hold him guiltless who takes his name in vain" (Exod. 20:7).

◇ **4.**
Would you say that electronic religion is primarily private? Is it possible for the electronic church to inspire *personal* but not *private* faith? Make some notes about your responses.

Looking at the congregation of which you are a part, do you think the people understand and practice this dictum: *Christianity is always personal but never private?*

◇ **5.**

List some of our actions that take the Lord's name in vain.

What about the first commandment, "You shall have no other god before me?" What actions violate that commandment?

◇ **6.**

As a practice in reflection, respond to these two questions:

1. At what moment during the past week did you feel closest to Christ?

2. At what time during the past week did you feel you were responding to God's call to be a disciple?

◇ **7.**

Go back in memory over the past few weeks, maybe the last two months, of your life. What has been your most glaring failure in Christian discipleship?

Get that experience clearly in mind.

Now, write a prayer of confession not only about that particular failure but also about the ongoing failure of your life to reflect what you affirm. Use the space on the next page.

But we don't have to speak to violate that commandment; we can violate it with our actions.   ◇ **5.**

The Emmaus movement is an interdenominational renewal movement sponsored by the United Methodist Church and The Upper Room. One of the most important dimensions of Emmaus is the follow-up to the Emmaus weekend, the ongoing life of those who participate. They are urged to be a part of a reunion group, a group of five or six or eight or ten people who will meet on a regular basis, hopefully weekly. It's the discipline of intentional growth and accountability, the mutual desire to be faithful disciples and share that pilgrimage with a few others. At the reunion group, the persons talk about their spiritual life, their study, and their action. Three questions they ask each other keep the Christian perspective clear. First, at what moment this past week did you feel closest to Christ? Second, at what moment during this week did you feel that you were responding to God's call to be disciples? Where did you participate in being the church, the heartbeat of Christ, this week?   ◇ **6.**

Now, hear this third question: When was your faith tested this week through failure?

That question puts things in perspective, doesn't it? When did we act out Christ's life in the world, and when did we fail to act out Christ's life in the world? Our lives must reflect what we affirm. ◇ **7.**

Only recently have I pondered a very significant aspect of Jesus' parable of the last judgment (Matthew 25:31-46). In that parable Jesus separated the sheep from the goats and directed some to depart "into the eternal fire prepared for the devil and his angels"; and others to enter the "kingdom prepared . . . from the foundation of the world." And you remember the basis for the judgment: "I was hungry and you gave me food, I was thirsty and you gave me drink, I was a stranger and you welcomed me, I was naked and you clothed me, I was sick and you visited me, I was in prison and you came to me" (vv. 35-36).

An interesting dynamic of this parable has really come through to me clearly recently. It was not just those who had not ministered to Jesus who did not realize that they had seen him hungry, thirsty, naked, sick, or in prison. Those to whom Jesus said, "I was thirsty and you gave me drink; I was hungry and you fed me; I was a stranger and you welcomed me . . ." asked him, "But Lord, when did we do this?" They also didn't know that they had seen Jesus hungry, thirsty, naked, sick, or in prison. But he said to them, "As you did it to one of the least of these . . . , you did it to me."

Do you get the connection I'm trying to make? Jesus also has said that we don't even know that we're saying, "Lord, Lord"— *but that he knows it; he knows it because we're saying it with our lives.*

So back to that point: our life must reflect what we affirm.

In *Have I Told You Lately . . .?* my friend Joe Harding has told of a cartoon that makes my point in reverse. The cartoon shows a psychiatrist's office. There are floor-to-ceiling shelves of books on each wall, along with a display of diplomas and credentials. A rather adequate-looking psychiatrist is there listening to a patient on the couch. Something, however, has startled the patient. His eyes are fastened on a corner of the room, and there is a look of horror and surprise on his face. The man is stunned! He can hardly believe it! The wallpaper is coming unglued. It is rolling up, revealing that the books and diplomas are just clever pictures on the wallpaper. He's there on the couch, desperately needing help, opening his life to this man who is revealed as a fraud! There are no words to the cartoon; you simply see the man's expression and you understand his predicament (Harding, p. 55).

It is a predicament faced by millions. Folks everywhere need the integrity of word and deed harmonized in a person. The world is too full of pretension, inundated with the superficial. Promises, promises—empty promises of fulfillment and meaning. We need desperately the powerful witness, the life-giving strength that comes from folks whose lives reflect what they affirm.

That's What the Man Said: "Not every one who says, 'Lord, Lord,' shall enter the kingdom of heaven."

I've noted two things. One, our Christian experience must be personal but never private; and two, our life must reflect our affirmation. Let me try to tie it together. I read a book back in 1969 which I have never forgotten. I hope I never do; I hope it will always haunt me. It was a book by the intriguing title *Include Me Out!* and the equally intriguing subtitle, *Confessions of an Ecclesiastical Coward.* Colin Morris, a Methodist preacher who now heads the religion department of the British Broadcasting Corporation in London, was then the president of the United Church in Zambia. In the book, he recalled that one day a Zambian dropped dead not a hundred yards from his front door. The pathologist said he died of hunger. In his shrunken belly were a few leaves and what appeared to be a ball of grass, nothing else. On that same day—the day the Zambian died of hunger—the *Methodist Recorder*, official magazine of British Methodism, came in the mail. Its columns were electric with indignation, consternation, fever, and fret over the postponement of the final report of the Anglican Methodist Unity Commission. Until that time, Mr. Morris said, he was enjoying the war over the union of two English churches. But the two scenes didn't go together—a man with a shrunken belly dying on his doorstep and two churches fighting over the disposition of unused communion bread.

Doesn't that paint the picture? Doesn't that say graphically what Jesus was saying: "Not every one who says to me, 'Lord, Lord,' shall enter the kingdom of heaven"? You see, the contrast is always there. A man with a shrunken belly, little children with

◇ **8.**

Spend some time now with this question: What other important messages are there in this word of Jesus besides the two discussed in this chapter: Christianity is always personal but never private, and our lives must reflect what we affirm. What would you add?

bloated stomachs, families living in pasteboard shacks, youth with no sense of direction, adults living in the snares of meaninglessness—all of this, yet Christians unaware of what's going on, too involved in theological debate, too intent on the reorganization of ecclesiastical structures, too busy rewriting their creeds and building their buildings and making sure everything is all right on the inside of the church.

But a nerve-jangling word breaks in upon our busy-being-religious life. "Not every one who says to me, 'Lord, Lord,' shall enter the kingdom of heaven, but he who does the will of my Father who is in heaven." *That's What the Man Said.*   ◇ **8.**

CHAPTER ◇ 13

The Poor You Always Have with You

The poor you always have with you. Have you ever quoted that word? Have you used the word to ease your conscience about not being concerned about the poor? If you haven't, surely you have heard others do so.

If you didn't know that this was Jesus' word, you knew somebody important said it, because you have heard it all your life. But Jesus is the source of the saying "The poor you always have with you." ◇ **1.**

That's What the Man Said, and we need to clarify what he meant.

First, we need to admit that Jesus was right. By that, I mean that his statement can be taken as fact. The poor we always have with us. The rising population of poverty-bound folks is the agony of our times.

Early Saturday night some weeks ago, I was at the church doing some preparations for Sunday morning. I left the church about 6:45, knowing that I had an Emmaus gathering at 7:30. Since it was rather dark, I was startled to see a woman coming toward me at the end of the sidewalk, running beside my office. She sort of stepped out of the shadows. She asked me if there was a pastor around. Her looks, her dress, everything about the situation momentarily caused me to want to say, "No, there's no pastor around."

Thank God, that temptation didn't live long. I told her I was one of the pastors. She said she had been in Memphis all day long, having hitchhiked that morning from Covington, Tennessee, and she had been trying to do some day-work to get some money to feed her children. I learned a part of her story at that point. She had three children and a husband who was legally blind. She had not been able to get any work, and she wondered if she could have $6 for a bus ticket back to Covington. She didn't know it, but I had only $17 in my pocket, and that's the only cash Jerry and I had together because we had pooled that cash before I had left home that evening. We had realized that I was going to be flying out the next day for a one-day trip to Lexington, Kentucky, and would not have a

◇ **1.**

Six days before the Passover, Jesus came to Bethany, where Lazarus was, whom Jesus had raised from the dead. There they made him a supper; Martha served, and Lazarus was one of those at table with him. Mary took a pound of costly ointment of pure nard and anointed the feet of Jesus and wiped his feet with her hair; and the house was filled with the fragrance of the ointment. But Judas Iscariot, one of his disciples (he who was to betray him), said, "Why was this ointment not sold for three hundred denarii and given to the poor?" This he said, not that he cared for the poor but because he was a thief, and as he had the money box he used to take what was put into it. Jesus said, "Let her alone, let her keep it for the day of my burial. The poor you always have with you, but you do not always have me."

—John 12:1-8

chance to get any money and would need a little bit of pocket money for that trip.

I asked the woman to wait until I went back into the church and called my wife. I thought I might pick Jerry up and take her with us to the bus station so that we might go from there to our meeting together. Rather pleadingly, the woman said, "Do you suppose that you could make me a sandwich?"

I called Jerry. We had been out of town on study leave for two weeks and Jerry had not had the opportunity to replenish our cupboards. All she had was the makings of a peanut butter sandwich. That would have pleased the woman, but I decided against it because Jerry was not ready and we were running out of time for me to get the woman to the bus station in time for her to catch the bus.

Driving downtown to the Greyhound bus station, I began to feel so sorry for her that I suggested that we run through a McDonald's and pick up a sandwich so that she could eat it on her way. She said, "If you don't mind, could you just give me the money that you would spend on the sandwich, and I'll keep it until I get to Covington, so I can buy a gallon of milk and a loaf of bread."

As we drove along, I learned this young woman's story. She was only twenty-five years old, but she had been married eleven years. Her husband is ten years older than she. She married at 14 to get out of the house because her father was an alcoholic who beat her mother and the children, and she felt that that was her only way out.

"Have you been happy in your marriage?" I asked. "Oh yes," she said, "very happy. Neither my husband nor I drink, and we've tried to work hard."

"What are you doing in Covington, Tennessee?" I asked.

"That's our problem. We were out in California and were doing pretty well. My husband had a job, but his sister who lived in Covington talked us into moving back here to live with them, so that we could be close as a family. She assured us that he could get a job here. Two months after we moved back, his sister moved away to Georgia. Two weeks ago, my father died, and even though he had mistreated me all my life, I had to help pay for his funeral. We just simply don't have any money. My husband gets a little check each month from the government; and lately, because we're out of work, I've been getting $121 a month as aid for my three children. We've simply run out of money, and there's nothing we can do."

By this time, we had arrived at the bus station, and my heart was sufficiently softened. I had $17 in my pocket, and I gave her $16. I wanted to keep a dollar to get back home and to get started on the next day. Driving home, I wished I had given it to her.

Jesus was right, "The poor you always have with you."

◇ **2.**

Poverty is a plague. Over thirty million people in America

◇ **2.**
Recall your latest personal encounter with poverty. Relive in your mind your reaction and response.

live below poverty level. One million people are homeless; they don't have a place to go or a bed to sleep in.

In New York City, there is an eighteen-year waiting list of 200,000 names for public housing. In my city of Memphis and Shelby County, one out of three families are victims of poverty. One-half of the children who go to public schools live in public housing, and there are 5,000 names on the waiting list for public housing.

My city, Memphis, has the third highest infant mortality rate in the nation, exceeded only by Washington, D.C. and Detroit, Michigan. Dr. Sid Wilroy, a geneticist and member of our congregation who does pediatric disease research and teaching, tells me that in 1987 the infant mortality rate for Tennessee was 7.6 per thousand. In our Shelby County the mortality rate is 6.3 per thousand for whites and 13.6 per thousand for blacks and other ethnic persons. Sid, with eyes misty out of deep concern and love, said that poverty is the primary disease we must fight. One out of three children who live will be on welfare by the time they become adults.

A revealing study of poverty conditions in my city talks about a "culture of poverty," a welfare cycle that has little children in its clutches and is almost impossible to break.

There are women and men and children walking the streets of our towns and cities by day and sleeping in alleys by night. There are older Americans living in the comfort of their homes but without supplies lining the walls of their pantries. There are working mothers with dependent children who cannot feed every mouth in the family and nonworking fathers who cannot stand the thought of facing their families without a check in their hands. We would not have to drive very far from the church most of us attend to be in the very heart of large pockets of poverty.

"The poor you always have with you." *That's What the Man Said*, and he was right.   ◇ **3.**

Let's move to concentrate on the whole story—to get the setting of this word of Jesus in mind. Jesus was having dinner in Bethany at the home of Simon the Leper, who had been helped by Jesus. His disciples and other friends were there.

In the midst of the celebration, Mary broke an alabaster jar of expensive perfumed ointment and anointed Jesus' head and feet. Thomas J. Gibbs, Jr. called her action *"memorable munificence."* Now those aren't everyday-speech words for most of us, but their strangeness may assist us in remembering what the story is all about. *Munificence* means lavish liberality. Out of gratitude for what Jesus had done for her, Mary took this expensive ointment— at the price of a working man's annual wage—and lavished it on Jesus.

Gibbs tells an old story about how, long before this anoint-

◇ **3.**
What do you know about poverty in your community, town, or city?
How many children are on the free lunch-program at school?
What percentage of your population is on welfare?
What is the infant mortality rate?
How many people are without jobs?
If you don't know, why don't you know?
Does what you know or don't know say anything about your concern?

◇ **4.**
Bountiful generosity, memorable munificence. What words would you add to describe Mary's expression of love?

◇ **5.**
Now when Jesus was at Bethany in the house of Simon the leper, a woman came up to him with an alabaster jar of very expensive ointment, and she poured it on his head, as he sat at the table. But when the disciples saw it, they were indignant, saying, "Why this waste? For this ointment might hve been sold for a large sum, and given to the poor." But Jesus, aware of this, said to them, "Why do you trouble the woman? For she has done a beautiful thing to me."

—Matthew 26:6-10

ing, Jesus had found Mary, this sister of Martha and Lazarus, living a dissolute life of harlotry in northern Magdala, a long distance from home. She was attracted to Jesus' message of love and forgiveness, and she responded. Jesus restored her to womanhood, to better things, and to her family. What may be an apocryphal story makes understandable and more plausible what we find this woman doing. This beautiful act, the meaning of which was known only to Jesus, was carried out without regard for her own feeling of embarrassment or humiliation and signified to him that Mary had not forgotten all that he had done for her.

That's the story, an unforgettable one. Of what? Bountiful generosity. Of what? *Memorable munificence.* ◇ **4.**

But there was another mindset there that day, the mindset of Judas—and though less pronounced, the mindset of the disciples. It was Judas's response to what Mary had done that evoked this word of Jesus. Judas asked, "Why was this ointment wasted in this fashion? Why didn't we sell it and give it to the poor?" In Matthew all the disciples raised the issue. ◇ **5.**

Not only the betrayer of Jesus but also his faithful ones often have a miserly mind. That was the mind that was being expressed there that day. They couldn't accept extravagant love being poured out by this woman.

Not only is the mind expressed by Judas and the disciples in response to the memorable munificence of Mary a miserly mind, it is what might be called a market mind.

The market mind is ever so closely akin to the miserly mind. In the words of Judas, it goes on quickly and always to say, "For this ointment might have been sold for more than 300 denarii and given to the poor." Life measured in the marketplace, weighed on the scales, and carefully computed as to its worth in dollars and cents!

The market mind has taken most of us in. George Bernard Shaw had a word of insight on the market mind when he said, "It is true that the world is governed to a considerable extent by the considerations that occur to stockbrokers in the first five minutes." (Gibbs, p. 43)

We saw that insight demonstrated on Black Monday in October 1987, when the stock market plunged, bringing jitters to the world.

A market mind attacks a whole system of welfare because some people misuse the system. Concentrating on those who may steal from the system, we often close our eyes to the nearly blind woman who is as honest as the day is long but would not survive without the meager $120 welfare check she receives.

A market mind angrily condemns food stamps because some person is cheating and drives off in a Cadillac with groceries purchased with food stamps, forgetting the bed-ridden man who will not eat tomorrow unless some volunteer delivers "Meals on Wheels."

A market mind sees the wheat rotting in some city in Africa, held up by political rivalry, and lets that sight blind it to the bloated bellies, the spindly arms, and the hollow eyes of starving children.

A market mind will condemn aid to dependent children, taking out anger on irresponsible parents who have been made irresponsible by an unimaginative system of what I call "welfare captivity." It will let anger at the system and those it sees as irresponsible blind them to little children and young people who will be enslaved by the same welfare mentality if we don't break them free.   ◇ **6.**

Have you ever noted in the story that Jesus said of the woman, "She has done a beautiful thing." He didn't say she did the best thing possible. Knowing him, I think he would have been moved deeply if Mary had given him the perfume and said, "Sell it and give it to the poor." He had given that command to a rich man, "Go, sell what you possess, and give it to the poor" (Matt. 19:21). But that's not what the woman did. She anointed Jesus with it, and Jesus said, "She has done a beautiful thing."

In the extravagant grace of the gospel, that's enough. We don't have to worry about whether it was the very best thing that Mary could have done. It was enough that it was a good and a beautiful thing to do, that she was free to do it, that she expressed her love for Jesus and anointed his body for burial. The market mind has difficulty understanding that.   ◇ **7.**

So that's the setting and the word to which Jesus responds! Mary's memorable munificence and the market mind of Judas and the disciples.

"The poor you have always with you." *That's What the Man Said,* and that's the word we are exploring.

Jesus was right. As we said earlier, the prevalence of poverty is the agony of our time. But let's loose Jesus from any binding suggesting that he was making a calloused, reference to the poor. If any one word characterizes Jesus more than any other, it is *compassion*, and that word gives us our clue to our ministry and our response to the poor.

Compassion is the heart, the core, of who Jesus was and what he was about, and Jesus reflected the heart of God. The witness of the Bible, so dominant that none of us can miss it, is that God is always on the side of the poor and the oppressed. I don't agree with every tenet of liberation theology, but I do agree with one claim that is at the heart of their understanding of the gospel. That claim is that God has a preferential option for the poor. You can't miss it if you read the Bible. All the prophets of Israel came out clearly at this point. They proclaimed, as the fires of God's judgment burned in their bones, that any nation and any individual who disregarded the oppressed and the poor would bring down the wrath upon them.

◇ **6.**
Read again each of the paragraphs that begins "A market mind . . . . " Put an x by any of these that reflect opinions you have expressed in the past few months.

◇ **7.**
Reflect on Mary's doing a *beautiful* thing and on the notion that perhaps it wasn't the *best thing possible*.
Do you excuse yourself from doing a beautiful thing because you feel incapable of doing the best thing?

◇ **8.**

What does the phrase "God has taken a preferential option for the poor" mean to you?

Is it true? Do you believe it? How might accepting it as true change your life? The ministry of your church?

◇ **9.**

If your judgment were today and you were judged on the basis of your concern for the poor, would Jesus say to you, "Come . . . inherit the kingdom," or "Depart from me."

When any of us oppress the poor, pay no attention to their plight, go our calloused way, we are opposing God; and we will pay a price.   ◇ **8.**

In his parable of the last judgment, Jesus is telling us that we can best show our devotion to him by the way we treat those in need. But he is saying something even stronger than that. He is saying that when we treat the poor badly, we're treating him badly; and when we are kind to the poor, we are kind to Jesus.

J. Ellsworth Kalas has stated the situation clearly:

> Poverty is terribly complex; so complex that we are tempted simply to throw up our hands and quit. It is partly a political problem, because governments and individuals use their resources to accomplish selfish ends rather than to solve the problem. It is partly an economic problem, in that we don't know how to use taxes fairly nor how to distribute what we have. It is partly a moral problem, because so many people prey on the poor, exploiting them for money and power. It is partly a spiritual problem: among the poor, in that they need to be stirred with the faith and energy to use what they have, and among the well-to-do, that they might be stirred to give of their time and money. But the complexity of the problem does not excuse us. I don't think God expects any one of us to solve the whole, ancient problem, but I'm sure He will hold us responsible for the small piece of the problem which is within our reach. Jesus agreed that the problem is so complex that we will have the poor with us always; but He also warned us that we will be judged, at least partly, on the way we treat the poor. (Kalas, February 10, 1985)   ◇ **9.**

My friend Harold Bales is minister of First United Methodist Church in Charlotte, North Carolina. That old downtown church has taken on new life and found new ministry and meaning reaching out to the poor. A part of that ministry involves street people. Every day the church has all sorts of people wandering around, people the likes of whom don't make up the membership of what has been an affluent congregation.

One day, one of those members, a well-dressed, well-educated, cultured woman, ran into Harold in the corridor, having passed many of these "not belonging" kind of people inside *her* church.

"What in the world are you doing?" she asked, obviously talking about the presence of all the street people.

"I'm trying to save people from hell," Harold responded.

"Oh, oh," the woman sort of stuttered. "I understand. We should be trying to save these people."

"No, I don't mean *them*," Harold said. "I'm trying to save *us* from hell."

Jesus would have applauded Harold, for Harold had gotten the message:

"Depart from me, . . . into the eternal fire prepared for the devil and his angels; for I was hungry and you gave me no food, I was thirsty and you gave me no drink, I was a stranger and you did not welcome me, naked and you did not clothe me, sick and in prison and you did not visit me." Then they also will answer, "Lord, when did we see thee hungry or thirsty or a stranger or naked or sick or in prison, and did not minister to thee?" Then he will answer them, "Truly, I say to you, as you did it not to one of the least of these, you did it not to me." And they will go away into eternal punishment, but the righteous into eternal life.

—Matthew 25: 42-46

Let's go back to the story in which Jesus gives us the word we are considering in this chapter. In Mark's presentation of this story, there is a word that John does not include. This is the way Mark 14:7 puts it: "For you always have the poor with you, and whenever you will, you can do good to them; but you will not always have me."

Note what is added. Yes, the poor are here, *and whenever you will you can do good for them*. Jesus is no longer with us in the flesh, but, according to him, whenever we will to do good for the poor, we will to do good for him. *That's What the Man Said!*

What you and I need to know is that not the failure of an economic system, or the evil of those who might exploit the poor, or even the failure of the poor themselves, or the overwhelming size of the problem leaves us any excuse when we stand before Christ. "The poor you always with you." *That's What the Man Said*. But he also added, "Whenever you will, you can do good for them." ◇ **10.**

◇ **10.**
As you look at your community and the needs of the poor around you, what is the *one* thing you can begin to do that will receive Jesus' affirmation, "You did it unto the least of these"?

CHAPTER ◇ 14

The Difference between Life and Death Is More Than a Tombstone

◇ **1.**

Now when Jesus came, he found that Lazarus had already been in the tomb four days. Bethany was near Jerusalem, about two miles off, and many of the Jews had come to Martha and Mary to console them concerning their brother. When Martha heard that Jesus was coming, she went and met him, while Mary sat in the house. Martha said to Jesus, "Lord, if you had been here, my brother would not have died. And even now I know that whatever you ask from God, God will give you." Jesus said to her, "Your brother will rise again." Martha said to him, "I know that he will rise again in the resurrection at the last day." Jesus said to her, "I am the resurrection and the life; he who believes in me, though he die, yet shall he live, and whoever lives and believes in me shall never die. Do you believe this?" She said to him, "Yes, Lord; I believe that you are the Christ, the Son of God, he who is coming into the world.

—John 11:17-27

In one of his sonnets, the poet Matthew Arnold tells how one day he met a college friend in the slums of London. This man was now a minister in that God-forsaken part of the city. Matthew Arnold was struck by the fact that here was the only happy face he had seen the whole day. When he asked his friend how it was that in this grim setting he could look so contented, so very happy, the reply came that he was nourished by Christ, the Living Bread.

Even though Matthew Arnold did not accept the Christian creed, this was his comment in his poem "East London":

O human soul! as long as thou canst so
Set up a mark of everlasting light,
Above the howling senses' ebb and flow,
To cheer thee and to right thee if thou roam—
Not with lost toil thou laborest through the night;
Thou mak'st the heaven thou hop'st indeed thy home.

Look again at that last line: "Thou mak'st the heaven thou hop'st indeed thy home." Restated, that clinching line might read in modern English, "The heaven for which we hope is already our home."

That's What the Man Said: "I am,"—present tense. "I am the resurrection and the life; he who believes in me, though he die, yet shall he live, and whoever lives and believes in me shall never die" (John 11:25-26). ◇ **1.**

Our challenge is this: We must take Jesus on his terms, or not at all! Above all the terms of Jesus towers this one—accepting his claim that he is the resurrection and the life.

The church and the Bible do not explain the resurrection: They are explained by it, and they start with it. There would have been no church and no Bible unless there had first been the fact of the resurrection. On Good Friday, Jesus died an apparent failure. His friends scattered, and his movement stopped, but on Easter he rose again from the dead, his friends reassembled, and his movement started up again, never to stop. The resurrection explains these things. It is an event of the same order as the creation itself. It inaugurates a new creation . . . .

Of himself, [Christ] said, simply as one can state a fact, "I am the resurrection and the life." This is one of the gigantic statements he sometimes made about himself. No other man ever made such claims for himself, unless he were beside himself. Who but God can call himself, "The Resurrection and the Life"? Those who would call Jesus merely a good man must reflect, "If he be no more than a good man, then he is not good at all: For these statements about himself are either unanswerably true, or they are inexcusably false. It appears that we must take him on his own terms, or not at all. To the best of our thinking, he is not merely man at his highest reaching up to God: He is God at his most merciful reaching down to man. (Shoemaker, p. 82)

So the big truth we consider in this chapter is this: *The difference between life and death is more than a tombstone—the difference is Jesus Christ!*

Pursuing this theme, let's think first about Jesus as the Resurrection and the Life as it relates to the possibility of our own ultimate resurrection, our eternal life, our resurrection from physical death. Go back to the first two lines of Matthew Arnold's poem:

> O human soul! as long as thou canst so
> Set up a mark of everlasting light,

If we can "set up a mark of everlasting light," then we don't have to feel hopeless. We don't have to struggle through the night, always verging on despair; we can live in confidence. For the Christian, the mark of everlasting light is that whoever lives in Jesus shall never die, because he is the Resurrection and the Life.

There's nothing distinctively Christian about belief in immortality; nearly all kinds of religion, and some people with little religion, believe in the survival of the soul. So, we either have to talk about Christian immortality or simply restrict ourselves to using the phrase *eternal life*. Christian immortality, or eternal life, is different from the natural wish for survival. Our faith in personal immortality is anchored in the resurrection of Jesus. We rely on Jesus' bracing words, "Because I live, you will live also" (John 14:19).

Shoemaker goes on to say that Jesus' resurrection made clear to us what Christian immortality is—"not the vague wandering on of lonely and orphaned spirits, floating somewhere between earth and heaven—but the continuation of ourselves, in communion with him and with one another. We're not a drop that falls into the sea of being and is lost in it; we are individual and responsible souls that return to their Creator." ◇ **2.**

◇ **2.**
What has been your understanding of the promise of resurrection? Have you distinguished between immortality and eternal life? Reflect on the difference.

Nothing is more threatened in our time than our sense of identity, the feeling of value and purpose. When we are reduced to numbers, it's not easy to hold on to conviction and feelings about eternal worth.

Some wag wrote a poem about it:

> The fellows up in personnel—they
>   have a set of cards on me.
> The sprinkled perforations tell
>   my individuality.
> And what am I? I am a chart upon
>   the cards of IBM.
> The secret places of my heart
>   have little secrecy for them.
> Friday my brain began to buzz;
>   I was in agony all the night.
> I found out what the trouble was—
> They had the paper clip too tight.

To our threatened identity, to our lack of conviction and feeling about eternal worth, the Resurrection speaks a powerful word; and the word is this: *the difference between life and death is more than a tombstone.*

One of the articles in the Apostles' Creed is: "I believe in the resurrection of the body, and the life everlasting." What do we mean by this? Again we call on Shoemaker to speak clearly.

> Do we mean that the particles of matter which make up our present bodies, and which will one day be dissolved into "dust and ashes" will come together again and form this same body over again? It cannot be. St. Paul says, "flesh and blood cannot inherit the kingdom of God." But he also declares that there is a "spiritual body," not a spirit only, but a "spiritual body." It is not exactly like the natural body, but it is more like it than pure spirit can be. He seems to be saying something that we moderns can best understand if we call it the survival of the whole personality—not just individuality, not just soul, but the whole self, with something that corresponds to the body of the present time. (Shoemaker, p. 83)

Our task is not to try to explain the resurrection of the body and the life everlasting; our task is to affirm this remarkable, life-changing promise of Jesus. "I am the resurrection and the life; he who believes in me, though he die, yet shall he live, and whoever lives and believes in me shall never die." *That's What the Man Said.*

Death is a great mystery that none of us will ever be able to probe. Yet Jesus said that we can trust the mystery because the difference between life and death is more than a tombstone.

I heard Henri Nouwen provide a beautiful metaphor that speaks about death and resurrection of the body. He said that every time he travels anywhere in the world and lands at some strange airport he has a fantasy that someone will be there who will say, "Hey, Henri! Welcome!" It will be somebody who knows him and who will welcome him with an embrace and a smile. Each time he waits for the voice, and each time he is disappointed. But then he says to himself, "It's all right. When I get home my friends or family will be there." Nevertheless, the fantasy persists. Every time he lands at a new airport he waits for the "Hey, Henri! Over here! How are you! Glad to see you!" Each time he is disappointed, but then he remembers that when he arrives back home his friends and his family will be there.

"So," said Dr. Nouwen, "heaven is going to be like that. God will be there, along with my mother, and my friends who have died, and they will say, "Hey, Henri! Glad to see you! How was it? Let's see your slides."   ◇ **3.**

Death is a great mystery. On this side of the boundary between heaven and earth, we invest a lot of fear and a lot of anxiety in the prospect of death and dying. The poet said, "There is no death, the stars go down to rise upon some other shore—and bright on heaven's jeweled crown they shine forevermore." He was only partially right. There is death, but for Christians death is swallowed up in victory, and we can shout, "Oh, Death, where is thy victory? O death, where is thy sting? . . . But thanks be to God, who gives us the victory through our Lord Jesus Christ" (1 Cor. 15:55). So mark it down: the difference between life and death is more than a tombstone.   ◇ **4.**

That's the word about eternal life and our resurrection from physical death. But there is more. "I am the resurrection and the life; he who believes in me, though he die, yet shall he live." *That's What the Man Said,* and the verb tense is present. *I am.* "I am the resurrection and the life."

Jesus' setting for this word, as you know, is the raising of Lazarus from the dead. Eugene O'Neill wrote a play about it entitled *Lazarus Laughed.* In a sermon Deryl Fleming retold the story this way:

> O'Neill has Lazarus laughing at death. At first the folk of Bethany laugh with Lazarus, their ears drunk with joy. Life has won and it's time to laugh. But laughing at death turns life upside down. It renders life on the old terms obsolete. It reverses everything so that things are no longer as they seem. Matters of grave importance cease to be important and a cup of cold water becomes a holy sacrament. Life as miracle is more than they with their will to live bargained for. Finally they put Lazarus where he belongs, back in the grave.
>
> Before they do, however, Lazarus, feeling their resistance, speaks to the people of Bethany: That day I returned did I not tell you your fear was no more, that there is no death? You believed then—for a moment! You laughed—discordantly, hoarsely, but with a groping toward joy. What! Have you so soon forgotten, that now your laughter curses life again as of old?

◇ **3.**

Do you have some metaphor for heaven or eternal life? Reflect upon death and resurrection. Think but also seek to *feel* what you think it will be like.

◇ **4.**

Lo! I tell you a mystery. We shall not all sleep, but we shall all be changed, in a moment, in the twinkling of an eye, at the last trumpet. For the trumpet will sound, and the dead will be raised imperishable, and we shall be changed. For this perishable nature must put on the imperishable, this mortal nature must put on immortality. When the perishable puts on the imperishable, and the mortal puts on immortality, then shall come to pass the saying that is written:

"Death is swallowed up in victory."

O Death, where is thy victory?

O death, where is thy sting?"

The sting of death is sin, and the power of sin is the law. But thanks be to God, who gives us the victory through our Lord Jesus Christ.

—Corinthians 15:51-57

Lazarus pauses, then speaks with sadness: That is your tragedy! You forget the God in you! You wish to forget! Remembrance would imply the high duty to live as a son of God—generously!—with love!—with pride!—with laughter! This is too glorious a victory for you, too terrible in loneliness! easier to forget, to become only a man, the son of a woman, to hide from life against her breast, to whimper your fear to her resigned heart and be comforted by her resignation! To live by denying life! Why are your eyes always either fixed on the ground in weariness of thought, or watching one another with suspicion? Throw your gaze upward! To Eternal life! To the fearless and deathless! The Everlasting!" (Fleming, pp. 100- 101)

That's the word for us: the difference between life and death is more than a tombstone. It is believing, staking our lives on the fact that eternal life is ours now.

"I am the resurrection and the life; he who believes in me, though he die, yet shall he live." *That's What the Man Said,* and when he said it, he asked, "Do you believe this?"

We must be careful that we see the full implications of that question. Howard G. Hageman writing in *Pulpit Digest* has put it in clear perspective: "Our Lord is not asking us whether we think that all this is so—an easy thing to do on a beautiful Easter morning when the blue sky seems a little nearer earth than at any other time of the year. Neither is he asking us whether we find ourselves sympathetic to the idea, as doubtless we all do. No, believest thou this? Are you willing to vote for it with your life? Are you ready to sink your foundations here? Are you able to trust the Easter Gospel even in the dead and cold of winter?"

What Easter as a present reality, what Jesus as the Resurrection and the Life for us *now,* means is *that we are set free from the fear of living* as well as set free from the fear of dying.

> The past is forgiven, thus we are
>   set free from sin and guilt.
> We don't have to cower back
>   in the shadows—afraid
>   of being found out.
> We are forgiven and our burden of guilt
>   can be cast aside.
> The binding chains of our fear of
>   tomorrow are loosened as
>   we are set free of anxiety about
>   *what might happen.* Concerns
>   of tomorrow do not cloud the
>   glory of today. No matter what
>   tomorrow may bring, he will be
>   with us. We sing, "I don't
>   know what tomorrow holds, but
>   I know who holds tomorrow."

To be sure, there will be the continued call of *seductive success* and *cheap gain*. The siren voice of lazy comfort and least resistance will beckon. Those who rush along at this mad pace to get ahead will want to carry us along with them.

So temptations to lesser life will persist. There will also be suffering and pain and loss of loved ones. But in it all our eyes must remain fixed on him whom sin could not break, hell could not hold, death could not capture. We must keep remembering that the difference between death and life is more than a tombstone.   ◇ **5.**

John Killinger tells a story about the seminary professor Joseph Haroutunian, who taught at the McCormick Seminary in Chicago. Haroutunian was an immigrant from Armenia to this country. When he arrived here, his accent was very strong. One day, a well-meaning friend took him aside and said, "Look, Haroutunian, your accent is a problem, but you can do something about that. Your name, though, is something else. Nobody can spell Haroutunian, and that is going to be a handicap to you professionally in this country. So why don't you change your name to Harwood or Harwell, something like that?"

Haroutunian looked at the man with interest and asked, "What do you mean?" The man said, "What does what mean?" "Those names, Harwood and Harwell—what do they mean?" The man replied, "Well, nothing. They're just easier to pronounce and to spell."

Then Haroutunian said this, "Back in Armenia when my grandfather was baptized, they named him *Haroutun,* which means 'Resurrection.' And when my father was born they named him *Haroutunian,* which means 'son of Resurrection.' My name also means 'son of Resurrection.' I am Joseph Haroutunian and I will be a 'son of Resurrection' all of my days."

That's the promise Jesus offers in his claim, "I am the Resurrection and the life." This is the birth sign of an Easter people: that we are sons and daughters of the Resurrection. We have no fear of living or dying. We stake our lives on the fact that eternal life is ours now. The difference between life and death is more than a tombstone. The difference is Jesus Christ, the Resurrection and the Life.   ◇ **6.**

◇ **5.**
If you believe that Christ gives you eternal life now, will that belief have specific implications for how you live? Describe these implications.

◇ **6.**
If you were asked to give the reasons why you believe in the Resurrection, what would you say? Write your responses here.

CHAPTER ◇ 15

You Shall Be My Witness

◇ **1.**

To them he presented himself alive after his passion by many proofs, appearing to them during forty days, and speaking of the kingdom of God. And while staying with them He charged them not to depart from Jerusalem, but to wait for the promise of the Father, which, he said, "you heard from me, for John baptized with water, but before many days you shall be baptized with the Holy Spirit."

So when they had come together, they asked him, "Lord, will you at this time restore the kingdom to Israel?" He said to them, "It is not for you to know times or seasons which the Father has fixed by his own authority. But you shall receive power when the Holy Spirit has come upon you; and you shall be my witnesses in Jerusalem and in all Judea and Samaria and to the end of the earth."

—Acts 1:3-8

A picture is worth a thousand words. True? Okay, let me try to paint the picture with words—fewer than a thousand of them. Better yet, you paint the picture in your mind as I tell the story told to me by Lycurgus Starkey, a United Methodist pastor.

An eighty-three-year-old grandmother stands in the checkout line of a K-Mart store. She chats with a young boy who is very proud of the $5.98 watch he has just purchased. Somewhere in their friendly conversation she asks the boy where he goes to Sunday school. He doesn't go. "Really? I think you'd like it," she tells him. "Could I call your mother and see if I can pick you up? We have a choir, too. The kids have a lot of fun."

So every Sunday this eighty-three-year-old woman picks up ten- year-old James for Sunday school and choir. His sister asks if she can come. Then the mother of the children wants to come to the children's choir concert. (There is no father in the family.) They all get to Sunday school and church in the old automobile of an eighty-three-year-old grandmother. Before long, the mother and her family find a church home.

Meanwhile, an eighty-three-year-old grandmother is back in K-Mart, at the pharmacy, in her apartment and her neighborhood, responding to Jesus.

Jesus' word which we consider in this chapter is the last one Jesus spoke to his followers before his ascension. Luke records that word for us in his record of the Acts of the Apostles: "But you shall receive power when the Holy Spirit has come upon you; and you shall be my witness in Jerusalem and in all Judea and Samaria and to the end of the earth" (Acts 1:8). ◇ **1.**

That's What the Man Said: "You shall be my witnesses." And that's what the eighty-three-year-old grandmother was doing in southern Illinois.

This was the last commandment that Jesus gave his disciples after his resurrection and prior to his ascension. "You shall be my witnesses." We hang on to the last words of our loved ones and friends, and we should! Just recently, a mother, still bearing the pain of her daughter's death, was sharing with me her anguish over her grandchildren, her deceased daughter's two girls. She told me with great feeling and with the freshness of a recent event what had happened eight years ago when her daughter was dying. She took her mother's hand and said with earnest pathos, "You'll take care of my daughters." And the mother responded, "Of course, I will!" And the mother, this grandmother, was hanging on to that word: "Take care of my daughters." This grandmother wanted desperately to be faithful to the last words of her daughter.

We hang on to the last words of loved ones and friends, and well we should. Certainly we should hang on to this last word of Jesus, his ultimate command to us. "You shall be my witnesses." *That's What the Man Said*. What does it mean for us? *To witness is the calling of every Christian.*

I heard a funny story about communication recently. A rather proper woman said to the clerk at the library: "I'd like a nice book to look at over the weekend."

"Here's one about a cardinal," the librarian said.

"I'm not interested in religion," the woman said.

"Oh, but the cardinal is a bird," the librarian said.

"I'm not interested in his private life," the woman said.

There's no problem of communication in this last commandment of Jesus. "You shall be my witnesses"; it's as straightforward as that. So nail it down. To witness is the calling of every Christian.

Do you know the name Billy Graham? Of course. But what about the name J. Wilbur Chapman? Do you know the name Billy Sunday? All these names are connected.

A Sunday school teacher, a Mr. Kimball, whose name is recalled only in forgotten books, in 1855 led a Boston shoe clerk named Dwight L. Moody to give his life to Christ. While preaching in England in 1879, Dwight L. Moody lit a fire of evangelistic zeal in the heart of a pastor of a small church. That pastor was Frederick B. Meyer.

F.B. Meyer became one of the great preachers of the world. While preaching on an American college campus, he was instrumental in bringing to Christ a student named J. Wilbur Chapman. Chapman became involved in YMCA work; through that involvement, God used him to reach a professional baseball player named Billy Sunday. Sunday became a world-known evangelist.

One of Billy Sunday's great revivals took him to Charlotte, North Carolina. Some businessmen of that city were so excited about it that they planned a second campaign and invited an evangelist named Mordecai Hamm to lead it. Hamm was hardly known, but during the Hamm revival meeting, a young man named Billy Graham heard the gospel and yielded his life to Christ.

◇ **2.**
Spend some time thinking about these two questions:

Who is the one person most responsible for your being a Christian, apart from your immediate family?

Who among the people you know is as intentional about witnessing as the eighty-three-year-old grandmother at the K-Mart in southern Illinois?

◇ **3.**
List three persons whom you think are effective Christian witnesses.
1._____
2._____
3._____
Now write a sentence or two about each of these persons, telling why you think they are effective witnesses.

Only eternity will reveal the tremendous impact of one Sunday school teacher, Mr. Kimball, who in 1855 led Dwight L. Moody to give his life to Christ.

Jesus anticipated that. That's the reason he said, "You shall be my witnesses in Jerusalem and in all Judea and Samaria, and to the end parts of the earth." To witness is the calling of every Christian. ◇ **2.**

Now a second simple truth: To fulfill our calling to witness, we have to have something to share.

Are you old enough to remember drummers, or have you heard about them? My mom and daddy have told me about drummers, salesmen who would travel from door to door in rural areas and small towns. These people, who sold merchandise from their covered wagons, were called drummers because most of them would pull into a town and beat a drum, a pot, or a pan until they had an audience. When they heard that sound, most of the residents knew that a rolling department store had come to town. Instead of going to the door of a farmhouse, the drummer would create his noise until the occupants came out to the road to see what kind of merchandise he had. A motto of the drummers was, "You can't do business out of an empty wagon."

That is a very descriptive phrase. You had to have an inventory of products if you were going to make a sale. Likewise, we Christians can't do business in our calling as a witness "out of an empty wagon." We have to have something to share.

What this calls for is very simple. We must know the Christ of whom we witness. We can't share with another what we don't have, anymore than we can come back from where we have not been. Human friendship gives us our cue. We like to talk about the friends we know and love. We like to introduce them to our other friends. The more we know and love them, the more free and spontaneous we are in introducing them, in wanting others to share in the joy of our relationship.

Do you get the point? To fulfill our calling to witness, we must have something to share; we must be comfortable in our relationship with Jesus. We must know him personally, and our relationshp with him must be making a difference in our lives. ◇ **3.**

The whole notion of being comfortable in sharing raises reservations about witnessing. Let's think about these reservations now.

The first reservation is this: Some of us are very hesitant to talk about hallowed things. The poet Emily Dickinson thought we should rightfully be hesitant, so she wrote, "People talk of hallowed things aloud, and embarrass my dog." Is it that we are embarrassed about the deep things of our lives; are we shy to share them? Is it because we think hallowed things are too private and personal? Whatever the cause of our hesitancy, we need to deal with it, because one of the great barriers to the Christian enterprise of witnessing is our reluctance to talk with others about God.   ◇ **4.**

My friend Donald Shelby tells of a little girl who came to her mother one day and said, "Tell me about God." The mother looked surprised and said, "Go ask your father." The little girl found her father, who was reading the newspaper. "Daddy, tell me about God," she said. The father did not put his paper down as he replied, "Go ask your teacher." The little girl went to her teacher the next morning and said, "Teacher, tell me about God." The busy teacher hastily suggested, "Go ask your minister."

So the little girl stopped by her church on the way home from school and told the secretary, "I'm here so that the minister can tell me about God." The secretary explained, "I'm sorry, but the minister is talking to God and cannot be disturbed. Can you come another time?"

The exasperated little girl, now on the verge of tears, protested, "Can he stop talking to God for a minute and talk to me about God?"

I really believe that people do want to talk about God. Once the silence is broken, once the superficial barrier is penetrated, people want to talk about things that matter, about their deep feelings about and yearnings for love, about death, about the purpose of life and where their lives are headed.

Don further relates how experts who study interpersonal communication tell us that most of our conversation consists of what they call "middle language," a language that is superficial and jocular enough to keep us disconnected from how we feel and from our serious thoughts. David Ignatow described it in this poetic dialogue called "Two Friends."

> I have something to tell you.
> I'm listening.
> I'm dying.
> I'm sorry to hear.
> I'm growing old.
> It's terrible.
> It is, I thought you should know.
> Of course and I'm sorry. Keep in touch.
> I will and you too.
> And let me know what's new.
> Certainly, though it can't be much.
> And stay well.
> And you too.
> And go slow.
> And you too.

So, Don goes on to say, we talk about the high price of lettuce, the playoffs and the Super Bowl, our diet, the stock market,

◇ **4.**
Are you shy in witnessing? Hesitant to share? Spend a bit of time examining why. What does reluctance to talk about holy things have to do with your reservations?

◇ **5.**
Go back to the three persons you named as effective witnesses and what you wrote about them. How do they talk about holy things? Does their effectiveness have anything to do with their willingness to focus conversation on important things?

◇ **6.**
Look at your own practice of witnessing. Are you intentional about it? Do you use the excuse of inadequate knowledge to keep from taking the initiative?

Are you afraid to share weakness or failure in your own life, because people might not think you are a Christian?

How comfortable are you in the assurance that you are Christian? That you have trusted Christ even though your experience may not have been a dramatic one?

Is being unsettled about your own Christian experience preventing you from witnessing to others?

the weather, the trivia at our work, taxes, the best car to buy, our aches and pains, our vacation plans, and what movie to see. "Every survey of people's conversations finds that these concerns and others like them dominate our verbal exchanges and our sharing with others, and only rarely do people speak of hallowed things," he says. (Shelby, January 17, 1988).

That's the tragedy. And that's the reason why many people never engage each other in real communication; they are hesitant to talk about hallowed things. ◇ **5.**

Sheldon Vanauken has written a marvelous book about his struggle with the faith and his conversion. He was influenced by C.S. Lewis. After he became a Christian, he wrote this confession in his book *A Severe Mercy:*

> But I—I a Christian! I, who had been wont to regard Christians with pitying dislike, must now confess myself to be one. I did so, with shrinking and pride. Indeed, I felt a curious mixture of emotions: a sort of embarrassment among my more worldly and presumably non-Christian friends, some of whom would have accepted my becoming a Buddhist or an atheist with less amazement, and a sort of pride as though I had done something laudable—or done God a favour. I was half inclined to conceal my faith, and yet it seemed to me that if I were to take a stand for Christ, my lord, I must wear his colours. (Vanauken, p. 101)

We must overcome our hesitancy to talk about hallowed things.

The second reservation that we have about witnessing stems from our feeling that we don't have anything to share.

Earlier, I made the point that if we're going to be witnesses we have to have something to share. I want to make it clear that feeling comfortable about our relationship to Christ does not mean that we feel we have a lot of answers. It doesn't mean that we don't have questions about our faith. It doesn't mean that we don't wake up at two or three o'clock in the morning sometimes and wonder where we are in our relationship with God and begin to question what God is doing in our lives. It doesn't mean that we are always bubbling over with joy because we're filled with the Holy Spirit.

What it means is that we are honestly seeking to cultivate our relationship with Christ, we have trusted him for salvation, and we are certain that it is only his grace that provides that salvation. It means that we are open and vulnerable, willing to confess that we are pilgrims on the road, not yet made whole but trusting him to complete the work that he has begun in us.

If we can have this attitude about the faith—that we are pilgrims, growing and struggling to incorporate the life of Christ in our lives—then we'll always have something to offer. ◇ **6.**

I like Lewis Grizzard, that sophisticated Georgia newspaper columnist who pretends to be very unsophisticated. Sometimes he offends me, and I think he does that deliberately. But he has a way of sharing life in a fresh way and getting at the heart of the meaning of life. In one of his columns, he reminisced about his childhood church:

What did they call Sunday night? MYF? We had a couple of rowdy brothers in town who broke into a store. They were juvenile offenders. Their punishment was to attend the Methodist Youth Fellowship for six months. First night they were there, they beat up on two boys and threw a Cokesbury hymnal at the lady who met with us and always brought cookies.

She ducked in time and then looked them squarely in their devilish eyes. Soft as the angel she was, she said, "I don't approve of what you boys did here tonight, and neither does Jesus. But if He can forgive you, I guess I can too." She handed them the whole plate of cookies, and last I heard, both are good daddies with steady jobs and rarely miss a Sunday in church. That was the first miracle I ever saw.

That woman provides the model. We don't have to worry about not having anything to share. If we love Jesus, if he's making a difference in our lives, if we care for others and believe that Jesus can make a difference in their lives, then we can share our love and our concern and, in doing so, share Jesus.

Now a final thought. If we are going to pay attention to Jesus' words and fulfill our calling to be witnesses, we must have what the old timers called a "passion for souls" and a plan for our witnessing. A passion and a plan. Unless we care enough to be deliberate and intentional witnesses, we are not going to be effective and fruitful in our witness.

Now I ask you honestly, and please be honest: Do you believe that Jesus has made a difference in your life—I mean really made a difference? Do you believe that Jesus can make a difference in the life of your friend or neighbor? Do you believe that? Do you believe that whether a person accepts Christ as Savior determines how and where he will spend eternity? Do you believe that? Do you believe that Jesus makes a difference as to where and how we are going to spend eternity? If you believe that, you will have a passion and a plan. You will be deliberate and intentional in your witness. Now please know, friends, that I not only preach to you, I preach to myself.

Let me confess. An incident has been haunting me now. About one o'clock one Sunday morning, the telephone rang. My heart beat faster; calls at that hour make me anxious. A woman's voice on the line asked if I were Pastor Dunnam. The fact that she said "Pastor" relieved me a bit; I knew she must be a stranger and probably was not calling about some Dunnam family concern. She poured out a sad story of a broken-down car, no money, no food, and no job. Headed for Oklahoma, she and her husband had slept in the car for two nights; and they were cold!

◇ **7.**

Look back over the past two or three months. Locate two experiences, one when you were deliberate and effective in your witness and one when you were ineffective and failed. Are there learnings from those two experiences that you can incorporate in a commitment to witnessing? Make some notes that will help you with a plan for intentional witnessing.

I had mixed emotions—sympathy for her and her husband and irritation that someone had given her my name. And she was calling me in the middle of the night, Saturday night, no less; and I had to preach on Sunday morning. I tried to deal with her over the phone, and I didn't do very well. I'm sure my irritation came through. I tried to come up with some resolution to her situation that would allow me to stay in bed and go back to sleep. I tried to convince the clerk at the Circle K store, where they were, to give her a tankful of gas and food and put it on my credit card. I gave him my credit card number, but he couldn't do that. It was against company rules; he was afraid that if he did it he would lose his job. So there was nothing to do but get out of bed and go.

Jerry was awake by then, and she decided she had better go, too. So we went. And I believe the cause was legitimate. We filled the car with gas, bought them some food, and sent them on their way with a bit of money and an expression of care and concern.

Driving home, I felt good—you know, I'd been a servant, and I could preach the next morning with power because I was authentically living the gospel—when Jerry shattered all those good feelings. We gave them what they needed, but we may not have given them what they needed most. Why didn't we tell them *why* we were willing to get out of the bed in the middle of the night and come to them—because we are trying to follow Jesus. Why didn't we pray with them and send them on their way with that sort of deliberate spiritual food? We didn't do it, and I haven't been able to forget that young couple. I hope they made it to Oklahoma, but I hope most of all that whoever helped them in Arkansas, or wherever else they made their plea, was more intentional and more verbal in their Christian witness than I had been. I hope that someone else who bought them a loaf of bread might have also broken the Bread of Life with them.

Now don't get me wrong! We don't always have to be talking about the faith, but we do need to have a passion for sharing the faith. We do need to believe that it makes a life-and-death difference. And we do need to have a plan—a plan for deliberately sharing the Good News. *That's What the Man Said,* and we had better listen to him! "You shall be my witness."   ◇ **7.**

Group Study Guide

Group Study Guide

When the group comes together for it's first meeting, spend some time getting to know each other. This is especially important if the group is "new." Ask each person to share something like: Why did you want to share this study? What is one of the happiest experiences you have had during the past month?

The leader should plan a specific way for opening and closing the meeting. Prayer and singing are important ingredients for this. Don't hesitate, though, to call the people to prayer in the midst of sharing if it seems appropriate. And how often is a hymn or song that people can easily sing just the right response to a significant time of sharing, even though it's not time for the meeting to close. So, plan the meeting, but be spontaneous and open to the Spirit's leading.

It is important that someone be designated to lead the discussion each week. The leader should plan ahead by looking at the suggestions and selecting the specific suggestion that he/she will use. Usually there will be more suggestions than needed, so it is important to prioritize according to what the leader feels will be most meaningful to the group.

Persons are most comfortable in a group where the "ground rules" are clearly understood. For instance, if you are going to meet for 1½ hours, be faithful to the time. Decide ahead whether refreshments will be served and define the kind of refreshments. It's usually best to have refreshments at the close of the meeting, so you can begin and close on time.

Prayer is an important part of group life. However, be sensitive to where people are in their prayer life. Whatever prayer experience the leader designs, make sure it will not be threatening to persons who may not have had much experience praying in a group.

In the sharing time, information is important, but personal response, feeling, and experience mean more than simply exchanging ideas. The leader should always seek to evoke from the participants—meaning, call to change, decision, feelings, experience—not just content. Also, be sensitive to each person, calling the reticent ones to share, and not allowing the more talkative to monopolize the time.

Chapter One

1. Let each person share the most helpful insight received from the study of this chapter.

2. Ask each person to name the three things they worry most about. Make a list of these to discover the most common. Talk about why these may be the most "popular" concerns.

3. Invite two or three persons to share their experience of "taking on excessive anxiety about things you cannot change."

4. Discuss "fear about living the Christian life." Is this a relevant issue in the group?

5. Does anyone in the group have an experience to share or a confession to make about "failure to live now"?

Chapter Two

1. What is the biggest question you have about the content of this chapter?

2. Invite as many as will to share some past decision which made a big difference in the direction of their life from then on.

3. Discuss whether persons shared choices and decisions that limited or restricted life, or enhanced and broadened possibilities.

4. In your spiritual discipline, with what area do you have the most trouble?

5. What essential physical discipline gives you greatest problems?

Chapter Three

1. Give three or four persons the opportunity to describe an individual who has had a "born again" experience.

2. What are the common characteristics in these experiences? Are the common characteristics essential to be a Christian?

3. Before studying this chapter, would you have thought of yourself as "born again"?

4. Discuss sin and *sin in your life*, in light of the definitions given.

5. Invite two or three persons to share an experience when they felt separated from God and then brought back to God.

Chapter Four

1. What new insight did you receive from the study of this chapter? How will this insight affect the way you think and live?

2. As many as will, recall and describe an experience within the past two months when you were a hypocrite because you didn't seem as Christian as you are.

3. Give three or four persons an opportunity to describe the person who is the most effective witness they know. After the descriptions, let the group discuss the characteristics of an effective witness.

4. Spend eight to twelve minutes talking about what it is about a so-called witness that turns you off? That attracts you?

5. Are there special persons or situations in your community which call for your group or your church to make a corporate witness? To be as Christian as you are? Spend the balance of your time talking about these questions.

Chapter Five

1. Let each person share the most recent experience they can recall when they apologized for being human.

2. Are there common ingredients in the sharing that indicate why we apologize for being human?

3. Discuss the notion that apologizing for being human is a violation of the gospel and a put-down of yourself.

4. Are there persons in the group who have had the experience of surrendering their limitations to Christ and having those limitations transformed or overcome with Christ's power? Share those experiences.

5. If you really believed Jesus' promise that "greater works than I have done will you do," what would you seek to accomplish immediately?

Chapter Six

1. Spend eight to twelve minutes talking about how, in your community, among your friends, popular opinion determines morality and/or duty. How does this harmonize with what you see happening nationally?

2. What are the three most crucial moral issues your community faces? Is your group or your church addressing these issues? What do you feel is your duty in relation to them?

3. Spend five or ten minutes talking about how a healthy sense of duty can save us from self-pity and self-righteousness.

4. Spend the balance of your time sharing your reflections on Nathan Soberblom's word, "Only with God's good hand and strict bridle can the soul be helped to give it's best."

Chapter Seven

1. Allow as many persons who will share how their family celebrated sabbath during their growing up years and how that has changed in their present family.

2. What new ideas or insights did you receive from this chapter?

3. Spend eight to twelve minutes talking about how we place institutional values above human values. Begin this discussion by inviting persons who feel they have been a victim of this displacement to speak. Keep the discussion as personal as possible—what *I* feel, what *I* have experienced, what *I* see. Be sure to look at the church in relation to this issue.

4. Ask persons to share how they use sabbath time other than Sunday worship.

5. Spend your remaining time talking about how to develop a lifestyle in which you spend time "doing nothing for God's sake and ours."

Chapter Eight

1. Invite three or four persons to share their experience of being chosen—not chosen by Christ but the feeling of being chosen.

2. Allow four or five persons to describe the person who for them reflects love most clearly. When these descriptions have been shared, let the group compile a list of words that characterize these persons. What about these persons is akin to the "love which God defines"?

3. Spend ten to fifteen minutes talking about predestination and "once saved, always saved." Be honest but not argumentative. Seek clarity of thinking.

4. Invite two or three to share their earliest memory of feeling they were chosen by Christ.

5. Invite as many as will to share how an experience of being loved by another person communicated the love of Christ.

Chapter Nine

1. What new insights did you receive from the study of this chapter? How will that insight affect the way you think and live?

2. Ask each person in the group to select the description of "how deep is down" on p. 71 with which he or she identifies most closely and share something about that experience.

3. Invite two or three persons to describe the person whose life verifies the truth that the circumstances of life are never as important as our attitude toward those circumstances.

4. Spend ten to fifteen minutes talking about the assertion that "the best way to believe Jesus and make his truth real in our life is to join Jesus in his continuing work of "overcoming the world."

5. Spend the balance of your time talking about how we are prone to live life as a "typographical error."

Chapter Ten

1. Invite as many people as will to share their most recent conversion experience—a time of specific change or new direction.

2. Allow two or three persons to describe the most humble person they know. After these descriptions, let the group discuss the child-like qualities in these persons that causes you to think of them as humble.

3. The marks of child-likeness are having the capacity to wonder, being capable of spontaneity, being comfortable with self, and being committed to change. Let each person take a minute or two to name the mark they need to cultivate most and why.

4. Spend the rest of your time with the group affirming the marks of childlikeness that you see in each other. Different persons will identify different marks in others. Be sure that every person is affirmed.

Chapter Eleven

1. Invite as many persons who will to share the occasion when Jesus hanging on a cross impacted their life most.

2. Spend eight to twelve minutes talking about the meaning of self-denial.

3. Give two or three persons the opportunity to share an experience when joy or purpose or meaning came to them as a result of willingly giving themselves, at some cost, to another or others.

4. Spend the balance of your time talking about what changes in attitudes, habits, actions, and/or lifestyle are required if you take Jesus' call to cross-bearing discipleship seriously. Keep the discussion at a very personal level.

Chapter Twelve

1. Spend five to ten minutes talking about the difference between personal and private religious experiences.

2. Let each person share the time during the past when he/she felt closest to Christ.

3. Let as many persons who will share an occasion during the past week when they responded to Christ's call to discipleship. . . . When they failed to respond to a call to discipleship.

4. Spend five to ten minutes talking about how we take the Lord's name in vain.

5. Close your time by asking a couple of people to share the prayers of confession they wrote about the ongoing failure of our life to reflect what we affirm.

Chapter Thirteen

1. What new insight or challenge came from your study of this chapter?

2. Invite three or four people to share confessions about having a "market mentality."

3. Spend ten to fifteen minutes talking about the assertion that "God has taken a preferential option for the poor." What does this mean for Christians in your community?

4. Invite three or four persons in the group to share experiences of being confronted by poverty and/or ministering to the poor.

5. Spend the balance of your time talking about what individuals, your group, and/or your church can do to reach out and minister to the poor in your community.

Chapter Fourteen

1. Spend ten to fifteen minutes talking about your reasons for believing in the Resurrection.

2. Invite two or three persons to share the experience that brought them a solid conviction about eternal life.

3. If there are persons in the group who have experienced the death of a parent, spouse, or child, let them share their experience of how and what comfort came to them.

4. Spend four or five minutes talking about the difference between immortal and eternal life.

5. Spend the balance of your time discussing the implications your belief in eternal life *now* has on how you live daily.

Chapter Fifteen

1. Ask two or three persons to describe their experience of being witnessed to effectively. Think especially of the person most responsible for your being a Christian (apart from your immediate family).

2. Ask two or three other persons to name and describe the most effective Christian they know. After the descriptions, let the group make a list of characteristics of these effective witnesses.

3. Spend ten to fifteen minutes talking about what you are hesitant to witness. What are the primary barriers preventing you from being an intentional witness?

4. Spend the balance of your time looking back over your entire experience together. Invite each person to share his/her most important learning and how it is impacting their life.

Notes

Sources quoted in this workbook are identified in the text by author and page number. If more than one work by the same author is cited, the title of the work is included in the citation. Bibliographic information for each source is listed below.

Blackwood, Andrew Watterson. *This Year of Our Lord*. Philadelphia: Westminster Press, 1943.

Brack, Harold A. "The Sabbath Was Made for Man" in *Pulpit Digest*, July-August, 1980.

Buscaglia, Leo. *Living, Loving, and Learning*. New York: Ballantine Books, 1982.

Chappell, Clovis G. *More Sermons on Biblical Characters*. New York: Richard Smith, Inc., 1930.

Chappell, Wallace D. *Receiving God's Fullness*. Nashville: Abingdon Press, 1960.

Cronin, A.J. *Adventure in Two Worlds*. New York: McGraw Hill, 1935.

Edwards, Tildon. *Sabbath Time*. New York: The Seabury Press, 1982.

Farmer, Herbert. *God and Men*. Nashville: Abingdon-Cokesbury Press, 1960.

Fleming, Deryl. "The Easter People" in *Master Sermons*. Volume 11. Royal Oak, MN: Cathedral Publishers, 1980.

Fosdick, Harry Emerson. *The Power to See It Through*. New York: Harper and Brothers, 1935.

————. *On Being Fit to Live With*. New York: Harper and Brothers, 1946.

————. *Living Under Tension*. New York: Harper and Brothers, 1941.

Fredrikson, Roger. *The Communicator's Commentary.*, New Testament Series. Volume 4. Waco: Word Books, 1983.

Gibbs, Thomas J., Jr. "Memorable Munificence" in *Pulpit Digest*, July-August, 1980.

Girzaitis, Loretta. "Sometimes, We Take the Initiative in Prayer" in *alive now!* July-August 1989.

Gossip, Arthur John. "The Gospel According to St. John" in *The Interpreter's Bible*. Volume 8. Nashville: Abingdon Press, 1952.

Harding, Joe. *"Have I Told You Lately . . . ?"* Pasadena, CA: Church Grove Press, 1982.

Johnson, Terrence E. "By Grace" in *Master Sermons*. Volumes 9 and 10. Royal Oak, MN: Cathedral Publishers, 1970.

Jordan, Clarence. *The Substance of Faith and Other Cotton Patch Sermons*. New York: Association Press, 1972.

Kalas, J. Ellsworth. "God and the Poor" (unpublished sermon) February 10, 1985.

MacLaren, Alexander. *Triumphant Certainties*. New York: Funk and Wagnalls, 1905.

Merton, Thomas. *The Seven Storey Mountain*. New York: Harcourt, Brace, Jovanovich, 1976.

Nelson, Culver. "Electronic Religion" in *Master Sermons*. Volume 13. Royal Oak, MN: Cathedral Publishers, 1982.

Ritter, William A. "Saviour by Storm Light" (unpublished sermon) September 11, 1988.

Saint, Steven. "A New Script for Martin Sheen" in *The National Catholic Reporter*, March 21, 1986.

Seymour, Robert E. "Apologizing for Being Human" in *Pulpit Digest*, November-December, 1980.

Shelby, Donald J. "Incognito" (unpublished sermon) January 16, 1977. "Speaking of Hallowed Things" (unpublished sermon) January 17, 1988.

Shoemaker, Samuel. "The Christ of the Resurrection" in *20 Centuries of Great Preaching*. Volume II. Waco: Word Books, 1982.

Trotter, Mark. "The Duty To Be Happy" (unpublished sermon) June 1, 1980.

Vanauken, Sheldon. *A Severe Mercy*. New York: Harper and Row, 1977.

Willimon, William. *With Glad and Generous Hearts*. Nashville: The Upper Room.

Woodson, Charles R. "Anyone for Calvary?" *Pulpit Digest*, April, 1965.